ON
AND OFF
THE
COURT

Red Auerbach
with Joe Fitzgerald

BANTAM BOOKS

TORONTO · NEW YORK · LONDON · SYDNEY · AUCKLAND

This low-priced Bantam Book
has been completely reset in a type face
designed for easy reading, and was printed
from new plates. It contains the complete
text of the original hard-cover edition.
NOT ONE WORD HAS BEEN OMITTED.

ON AND OFF THE COURT

A Bantam Book / published by arrangement with
Macmillan Publishing Company

PRINTING HISTORY
Macmillan edition published 1985
Bantam edition / December 1986

Published simultaneously in the United States and Canada

Bantam Books are published by Bantam Books, Inc. Its trademark, consisting of the words "Bantam Books" and the portrayal
of a rooster, is Registered in U.S. Patent and Trademark Office
and in other countries. Marca Registrada. Bantam Books, Inc.,
666 Fifth Avenue, New York, New York 10103.

PRINTED IN THE UNITED STATES OF AMERICA

KR   0 9 8 7 6 5 4 3

This is not a basketball book, though there's plenty of basketball in it because basketball's been my life. It's more of a "people" book. That's really the story of the Celtics: People working together, paying the price, accomplishing what they set out to do. I'm not saying we haven't made mistakes. We've made our share. But we've done a lot of right things, too, and maybe there's something to be learned from the success we've enjoyed.

—Red Auerbach

RED AUERBACH
ON & OFF THE COURT
IS A WINNER!

"*On & Off the Court* is the next best thing to watching the Celtics play."

—Senator Ted Kennedy

"The cantankerous Auerbach gives us 'The World According to Red.' Great reading for sports fans."

—*Booklist*

"I could hear Red's voice on every page. It's the Red I know. He's tough, but he's also fair and compassionate. . . . I've been a fan of his for a long time, and this book makes me respect him all the more."

—Bobby Orr

"Readers will be continually impressed by Auerbach's dedication to his players, coaches, and fans, and many will regret that such fierce pride is missing from so many of today's super-monied arenas. Certain to be a favorite among all sports fans, this book is highly recommended for sports collections."

—*Library Journal*

"The builder of the Boston Celtics dynasty which won eleven championships in thirteen years here tells how he did it, offering his philosophy of life together with his prescription for success on the court."

—*Publishers Weekly*

To my wife, Dot.
To my daughters, Nancy and Randy.
To my granddaughter, Julie.
To the memories of my father and mother,
Hyman and Marie Auerbach;
of my father- and mother-in-law,
Dr. and Mrs. Edward Lewis,
and their son, Dr. Edward Lewis, Jr.;
of Walter Brown and Bill Reinhart.
And to all of the great athletes
and other people who have played
such important roles in my life.

Contents

Acknowledgments

The authors wish to thank the following individuals for their invaluable assistance in the preparation of this book: Jan Volk, Bob Richards, John Cronin, Charles Pierce, Mike O'Connor, Alan Weiner, John Hinchey, Dave Farrell, Navy Labnon and Lloyd Rines.

We also wish to thank our editor at Macmillan, Jeff Neuman, for his many thoughtful suggestions and his helpful advice. We knew we were in good hands.

Finally, we especially want to thank our literary agent, Larry Moulter, who gave birth to this project with a vision and an enthusiasm that he then imparted to everyone else who came aboard along the way. Thanks, Larry.

Introduction

"You're a champion. And it shows."

I'd heard dumb questions before, but this one really got to me.

They honored me in Boston last winter with a very emotional weekend. It began with a ceremony at the Garden on Friday. Almost all of my guys were there: Cousy, Russell, Havlicek, Heinsohn; Ed Macauley, Frank Ramsey, KC Jones, Sam Jones, Jo Jo White; even the fellows we picked up late, like Wayne Embry, Charlie Scott, Pete Maravich. They all came, about 30 of them, and they played in an oldtimers game the next afternoon. Then we had a party Saturday night—black tie!— which raised about $500,000 for a fund that's been set up in my name to subsidize sports for kids in the city.

To top it off, they're putting a statue of me right in the heart of Boston alongside the statue of James Michael Curley, the legendary "Mayor of the People."

The party's almost over when this TV crew asks me for an interview. The first question is, "How does it feel to be a recipient of this—do you deserve it?"

I looked at the guy. I couldn't believe it. "You know, I don't want to insult you," I said, "but that's a dumb question."

He kind of laughed. "Well, you've said that to me before."

"I know," I said, "but this really *is* dumb!"

Okay, maybe I was rough, but he'd put me on the spot. Actually, the question was entirely reasonable; it was the same one I'd been asking myself all weekend. No one ever expects to be honored like that. Certainly not while he's alive. All the statues around town have been put up for dead men. So, sure, you have to ask yourself: Did I do enough to merit something like this?

You can dream of making it into the Hall of Fame. You can dream of receiving accolades and awards. You can even dream of winning championships. But statues? Downtown? No way. That's just not a part of your dreams.

I've never thought of myself as an immortal, statue or no statue. We'd be winning championships every year, and just to get myself back down to earth I'd say to my wife, "You know, Dot, I just looked through the want ads and there's not one damn job I'm qualified for. I'm not a mechanic. I'm not a carpenter. I'm not a bricklayer. I'm not an engineer. So if, all of a sudden, there was no basketball tomorrow, what would I do?"

Contrary to what my image might suggest, I've never gone looking for publicity. Never. I found out that if you keep a low profile—approachable but not too approachable, not always available but available when necessary—when you do have something to say people will listen, and they'll print it.

As I looked around at all those familiar faces that Friday night in the Garden, and looked up at all those flags we had won together, I'll tell you what I did feel: I felt that all of the things I so deeply believed in— loyalty, pride, teamwork, discipline—had been proven correct, over and over.

I'm proud of what we've accomplished as an organization. I'm proud of what the Celtics have come to stand for. Because of technological advances in the media, we've become more than just a national team; the Celtics are an international team today. We receive mail from all over the world, from people who've heard of what we've done, from kids, coaches, fans. That gives me a great feeling. It's more than just winning; it transcends winning. It goes right to the heart of what we like to think we're all about.

When you talk about the Celtics' tradition, it goes beyond winning, although that's certainly a big part of it. It's more than just how you play. It's how you feel, how you act, how you carry yourself and conduct yourself. You're a champion. And it shows.

Officially, I've retired as general manager. As soon as you say "retirement" there's a tendency for people to think, Oh, he's an old man. What the hell does he know? But if he comes to the game let's introduce him to the crowd, give him a hand and make a big deal of it . . .

It's not that you're unwelcome. That's not the word. You're tolerated. I never want to feel tolerated. I still want to feel stimulated. That's why I teach a course at Harvard. That's why I'm still the president of the Celtics.

The thing that bugs me about retirement—and I'll get into this later—is that it has come to mean you've been farmed out, excommunicated; you're now looked upon as some poor bastard just waiting to die.

Well, I've got no intention of dying. Not yet anyway. What I do have—and maybe this comes with getting older—are thoughts on today's game and the world in which it's played, thoughts based upon the experiences we've had in Boston and upon what I believe to be time-less values.

This is not a basketball book, though there's plenty of basketball in it because basketball's been my life.

It's more of a "People" book.

That's really the story of the Celtics: People working together, paying the price, accomplishing what they set out to do.

I'm not saying we haven't made mistakes. We've made our share. But we've done a lot of right things, too, and maybe there's something to be learned from the successes we've enjoyed.

I'd like to think so, anyway.

ON
AND OFF
THE
COURT

1.

Philosophies and Flashbacks

"Nobody's ever gonna hit me first again."

I'm just the opposite of the way my father was. He was a very friendly guy. He liked people. People liked him.

In his own quiet way he was a very bright guy. He would have made a magnificent teacher. He used to tell me stories about the old country, how he'd learned to read and write there, how he'd travel around by train, making friends with all the conductors; how they got to like him and didn't charge him the penny it would have cost to ride to school.

His home was in Minsk, over in Russia, but he left there when he was 13 years old. His mother and father—my grandparents—put him on a ship bound for America, along with his brother. They wanted their kids to have a shot at a better life and to be free from the anti-Semitism that threatened all Jews in Europe at that time.

I don't know too much about that period of time in his life. He seldom talked about it. I just know he was a hard-working, enterprising guy who migrated to Brooklyn, rather than to the East Side where most of the other immigrants headed, and while I can't put my

1

hand on a single incident or event that made me feel this way, I know I always had a great desire to please him, to make him proud of me.

Before he saved enough money to open his own dry cleaning shop, he worked for someone else's plant on a commission basis. He had a route that went all over New York, from the 50s down to the lower East Side. We'd make plans each morning for where we'd meet that afternoon, and when school ended I'd grab a trolley and catch up with him on the East Side, or maybe take the subway uptown to the spot that we'd agreed upon. And I'd help him.

I'll tell you what kind of a guy he was. We'd be down by the docks on 46th Street between 11th and 12th Avenues. Hell's Kitchen, you know? A tough area, right next to the Hudson River. The gangsters there all liked my father. I remember one in particular. They called him Swanee. He *was* later electrocuted. He thought my father was a decent guy—a nice guy—so he and his friends sort of protected him whenever we were in the area. See, my father had a way of communicating with the common man. He *was* a common man.

Years later, when I had settled in Washington, D.C., he'd come down for a visit. He'd take a walk or go to the store, and all of a sudden he had new friends. You know what I mean? I can go into a town and stay by myself for three days and be happy. Not him. He liked people.

He lived to see the success I enjoyed in the NBA, and that meant a lot to me because he never approved of all the time I spent playing the game as a kid. It wasn't that I wanted to prove him wrong; I just wanted him to see that I was right, that my time hadn't been wasted.

I can't remember when I didn't love basketball. There wasn't a tree in sight at my school. Everywhere you looked, all you saw was concrete, so there was no football, no baseball, and hardly any track there. Basketball was our game, and I played it every chance I got. From elementary school on, I was one of the best players in the area.

But my father didn't know what it was to be a kid in this country. He never had a moment of youth here. It made no difference what your age was—10, 12, 14—when you stepped off the boat as an immigrant in those days, you were expected to be a man. There was no such thing as going to school for people like my father. He had come here to work, to make some money, to create a life that wouldn't have been available to him back in his homeland. That was what America was about; it wasn't playing games and having fun. It was being industrious enough to stand on your own two feet, to become self-sufficient, to someday start a family and be able to provide security for your kids.

Those were my father's goals in life and, to his credit, he achieved them. He saved enough money to buy a little restaurant in Manhattan, right across from Radio City. The owners offered him the entire building for $11,000, and he wouldn't touch it. Can you imagine what that would be worth today? After hearing the story, years later, I never let him forget it. It became a standing joke between us.

Just before I was born in 1917 he sold the restaurant and bought a little deli in Brooklyn. I used to love watching him cut those big loaves of bread: Zoom, zoom, zoom! Same thing with cutting meat. He was all business, and so good with his hands. But he never had time to build things, to have fun, to indulge in recreational pursuits. He was always too busy working, making life comfortable and secure for the rest of us. When he came home at night, he was tired. I could see it, and it just deepened my respect for him. That's why I was always willing to pitch in and help whenever he needed me.

The only disagreements we ever had involved the time I spent on basketball. It wasn't that he disliked sports, although he was never what you'd have called a fan. He knew enough to take his kids to watch Ruth and Gehrig play every once in a while; he realized that was part of being an American father.

In his mind I was not the son who'd go to college. That was traditionally seen as the goal for the oldest son. That's how folks who came here from the old country felt: The oldest son was the one to get the education. Walter Brown, the Celtic's founder, once told me it was the same way in old Irish families.

My older brother Victor was the student. My marks weren't as good as his and, besides, I was bigger and stronger, more suited for physical work. But I wanted to be a teacher and a coach. That was my dream, and I knew the only way I could hope to fulfill it was by earning a basketball scholarship.

"Pop," I told him, "I don't know if I'll ever be good enough to play my way through school, but I've got a decent shot at it, so I've got to try. It's important to me. It's something I *must* do."

Once he saw that I had made up my mind, he didn't try to hold me back. In fact, he sort of came over to my side and encouraged my ambitions. He could have said: "Nothing doing. I *need* you to help me feed the others." He could have placed that kind of pressure on me, but he didn't. That wasn't his way. I was his son, and if this dream of mine was all that important to me, then no one was rooting any harder for it to come true than he was.

And it did come true. I got a scholarship to Seth Low Junior College, which was affiliated with Columbia University, and then Bill Reinhart, the coach at George Washington Universty, offered me the chance to play for his team on a full ride.

I'll always remember the first time my father ever saw me play; he'd never been to a basketball game before. I was playing for Seth Low. I was the ballhandler, and the other team was set up in a zone. So I spent most of the night in the backcourt, passing here, getting it back, passing there, keeping the ball on the go.

"Well," I asked him after it was over, "how'd you like it?"

"It was all right," he said, "but I can't understand one thing. You're in the living room, and all the action's in the kitchen. No wonder you couldn't score!"

I never forgot that. It was a great observation from someone who'd never seen a game before and who, of course, had no appreciation of what it meant to spend the night trying to beat a zone.

Later in his life, when he began going to Madison Square Garden to watch my clubs play the Knicks, he became a pretty good fan.

All those hours I'd spent as a kid shooting a ball through a hoop had paid off handsomely. I'd made my dream come true through hard work and dedication. I'm sure that pleased him more than he ever let on, because it was the same thing he'd done in his own life.

I borrowed money from my father only once. He loaned me $3,000 so that I could buy my first house, and I paid it back in about a year and a half, though I really didn't have to.

We'd kid a lot about money. I can remember going back to New York after he'd retired and giving him a hard time about my sister Florence. There was a period of time there when she didn't have a lot. Her husband Sid—a super kid; he took better care of my mother and father than I did—was driving a cab, which my father had loaned him the money to buy. Sid ended up doing very well, and he and Flo really looked after my folks.

So one day, while I'm home for a visit, I pull my father aside.

"Hey, why don't you buy Flo a car?"

"For what?"

"For what? For driving you and Mom around town all the time, that's for what."

"Mmm. Maybe."

"Do you want me to make you look cheap? Do you want *me* to buy her a car? Okay, I'll buy her a car."

He started to laugh. "All right," he said. "All right! I'll buy her the car."

You could reason with my father. It wasn't that he was tight. He was just a hard worker from the old school who, for instance, couldn't understand spending a lot of money to eat in a restaurant when there was plenty of food at home.

I'll never forget one lesson he taught me a long, long time ago. I was just a kid at the time, traveling the New York subways where they had—and still have—all these hawkers pushing all kinds of goods at you.

One particular guy was selling socks. They were all wrapped up in brown paper bundles, tied with a piece of string. He was charging 5 cents a pair, but the catch was that you had to buy at least six pairs. Well, I figured to myself, "This is a hell of a bargain." So I bought *two* bundles at 30 cents each. Okay, I know that 60 cents doesn't sound like such a big deal today, but, believe me, to a kid growing up in the early days of the Depression, 60 cents was a very significant amount of money, certainly not to be parted with lightly.

But everyone needs socks, right?

So I took my big purchase home with me, and I felt pretty shrewd—until I opened the bundles and discovered that no two socks matched! They were all remnants from some factory.

One particular vendor tried to interest me in a $3 Indian-head ring. I really wanted one; they looked sharp. But I didn't have the dough. So I tried to borrow it from my father, and when I told him what I wanted it for, he absolutely refused. I kept badgering him, asking him to advance me the money from my allowance, but he was adamant; "The stuff has to be junk!" he insisted.

No money, no ring. I was mad.

A couple of weeks later I was walking down a street on the East Side and what do I see? A whole tray of Indian-head rings. Some guy's selling them for 25 cents apiece, the same ring I almost paid $3 for!

That time I didn't get burned, thanks to my father. I still think of things like that when I'm offered deals today. I learned a lot from him, but most of all I'd like to think that I've got a little bit of his integrity.

Sometimes my wife gets embarrassed when she thinks I don't act nice enough in public. I try to tell her, "Dot, you can't be Mr. Nice Guy all the time. Show me a guy who can't say no and I'll show you a guy who's got problems. Lots of problems."

Do I walk around with a chip on my shoulder? I don't think so. Do I have a combative personality? I guess so. Sometimes. But I'm not sure that has anything to do with the way I grew up.

I do remember this, however. Our neighborhood was a real melting pot: Irish, Polish, Jews, lots of Italians, some blacks. It was all mixed up. And every once in a while, when a kid had nothing better to do, you'd hear: *"Hey, you lousy Jew!"* Oh yeah. I heard that. Especially on certain streets.

One time a guy was giving me some crap. It was one of those things: *"You dirty Jew!"* So I started jawing back at him, and the next thing I knew he banged me right in the face. Then he beat the hell out of me, because once he got that first shot in, it was all over.

I don't know how old I was then; about 10, I guess. But I never forgot it. After that, I didn't get hit first anymore! I remember thinking to myself that day: *Nobody's ever gonna hit me first again. I'll hit first and take my chances later!*

That was more than 50 years ago, but it's still fresh in my mind today. I learned early to stand up for myself and for what I believed in.

When I was an acting petty officer in Navy boot camp at the Great Lakes Naval Training Station in 1943, there was this big redhead on the rowing team, a strong kid who'd come walking into the mess hall and go right to the front of the chow line. One day he stepped in front of me. I told him: "Hey, stay in your place. The fact you've been out there rowing all day doesn't mean a damn thing to me."

He started giving me some abuse, so I said: "Okay, let's go to the gym."

They gave us these 16-ounce gloves. I couldn't hurt him, but I got my satisfaction because he couldn't hurt me, either. And he didn't bother me anymore after that.

Later, at Physical Instructors School in Bainbridge, Md., I came across a guy named Johnny Rigney, a great pitcher for the White Sox. In those days baseball players called everybody "Bush." It made no difference who you were; you might have been an All-American with nine degrees, but if you weren't a big league baseball player they all called you "Bush."

Well, I didn't know that at the time. So one day Rigney's walking by and he says, "How are you doing, Bush?"

I didn't like it, so I said: "You big sonofabitch, let's go out back and we'll see who's *bush!*"

He started laughing, and once I understood what the big joke was, I laughed, too. Johnny and I went on to become real good friends.

I was never ashamed of where I came from, or of the house we lived in, or anything like that. All of the kids I hung around with came from similar backgrounds.

But I never wanted to give anyone the impression that I was an uneducated "Thoity-thoid Street" guy, you know what I mean? I didn't want to be stereotyped as a typical wise-ass Brooklyn character. I didn't want to be stereotyped as a typical anything.

This really came home to me when I was a senior at Eastern District High School. I was captain of the basketball team. In fact, I was named All-Brooklyn, Second Team, which some of my Celtics used to laugh about until I informed, say, John Havlicek, that there were more outstanding schoolboy stars in Brooklyn when I went to school than there were in all of Ohio when he was all-state. It was a significant accomplishment.

One day some kids came up to me and suggested that I run for president of the student body. No athlete had ever run for that office before. We lived in our world, and the real serious students, the ones who always ran for president, lived in theirs. But I liked the idea, so I said okay and we put together our own ticket: *Auerbach, Rizzo & Rabinowitz!* I'll never forget it. We had a campaign fund of $5, which we used to print our names on some blotters.

Now I had to get up and give a speech in front of

the whole school assembly. My knees were shaking, my voice started to crack, and I can remember feeling kind of sorry for myself because I felt so totally inadequate. I wasn't confident in my ability to pronounce words. The guy running against me, meanwhile, was completely at ease, and he made me look like a bum. His name was Saul Ritter, and he went on to become a very famous cantor. We'd bump into each other in later years and laugh when we looked back. But it was no laughing matter to me then. I think half of my speech was delivered in a falsetto. It was awful. And to make matters worse, I won—which, I then discovered, meant my first duty was to read the Bible at the next school assembly! Again, my knees began buckling and I started feeling squeamish. I got through it, somehow, and they never asked me to do it again.

That whole experience had a big effect on me. I'd say things like "foist" and "thoid" back then, and since everyone around me spoke the same way I never felt ostracized. But when I'd go to the movies I'd notice that other people didn't talk the way we did. Their manner of speaking was clearer. Without anyone suggesting it to me, I simply knew that this was an area of self-improvement that I had to do something about.

The next year, when I enrolled at Seth Low Junior College, I signed up for a course entitled "Voice and Diction." The woman who taught it gave me some valuable tips, such as picking out one person in the audience, addressing my remarks to him, and projecting my voice so that he could hear me. And she taught me to feel confident in my subject matter, because the audience wanted to hear me, and it obviously didn't know as much about the subject as I did.

I learned how to make people listen to me by varying the way I used my voice: Raising it, then lowering it, then raising it a little bit more, always keeping an eye out for reactions. This would become extremely important to me as a coach, because good communication is essential. It is equally essential for a teacher, which is what I originally wanted to become.

I didn't know what I'd be doing when I took that

course at Seth Low. Not for certain. All I knew was that whatever I ended up doing, I wanted to feel better about myself and about the image I projected.

I was stationed in Norfolk, Va., during World War II and I got to be friendly with Phil Rizzuto, who was also stationed there. We'd spend hours discussing sports, which invariably led to talks about his manager, Joe McCarthy, and the Yankees.

Phil told me how McCarthy was vitally concerned about the Yankees' image. It's funny how you remember things. We were eating spare ribs that day, and the more Rizzuto talked, the more fascinated I became with what I was hearing. He said Joe believed the way a team conducted itself off the field had a lot to do with the way it performed on the field. He told me how McCarthy would take kids from farms and ghettos and pull them aside, teaching them how to tip properly in restaurants, how to dress properly in public, how to act properly in places like hotel lobbies.

The idea made a lot of sense to me. A guy like DiMaggio really did look and act like a champion. So it only made sense that if you could get an entire team to look and act the way DiMaggio did, you'd have a hell of a team on your hands. And I remember thinking right there, over spare ribs with Rizzuto, that if I ever got to the professional coaching level, I wanted my ballclubs to look and act like champions, too.

Later I got to know DiMaggio, and Yogi Berra, too, and, like Rizzuto, they told me all about McCarthy and his philosophy. One day, long after we'd started winning championships in Boston, someone wrote an article in which I mentioned the influence McCarthy had had on my career and how I felt about the man. He was an old man then, in his 80s, and he called me up to thank me for what I'd said. What a thrill I got out of that.

I still think image is important. I've never changed my feelings along those lines. That's why I was kind of upset when Bill Russell and then Tommy Heinsohn relaxed our dress code when they succeeded me as coach. It's funny, but a kid who grows up in poverty dreams of the day when he can afford a cashmere sport coat or a cashmere sweater. Then he achieves tremendous success, and what does he do? He doesn't buy cashmere stuff. Now that he can have it, he doesn't want it. So he goes back to wearing dungarees and sneakers. Look at your big movie actors. When you meet them on the street, what are they wearing? Dungarees and sneakers. I don't go along with that. I still think it's important to have some respect for yourself and your public image, and to project a little class.

The first time I noticed that trend was when the great Knickerbocker team of the early '70s came to power. We played in New York on a Saturday night, and then we all flew back to Boston for a Sunday afternoon game. I saw them in the airport and I couldn't believe it. One guy's wearing sneakers with no socks, someone else is wearing a T-shirt, another guy's dressed in Army fatigues. Thank God, I thought, for Walt Frazier and Henry Bibby. Those two guys were dressed immaculately. I'd have been proud to have them on our side.

I caught some heat last winter when they threw that big time for me in Boston. Almost all of my old players came back, and they staged an exhibition game: my side against Russell's side. Many of these guys were grandfathers now and hardly in competitive shape, so I told them, "Look, if you can't do much, just jog up and down the court once, take a shot, make a pass, and I'll pull you out." I didn't want them to make fools of themselves. But that didn't mean I wasn't playing it straight, and I became upset when I thought the referees were turning it into a joke. So I raised hell, and the next day everyone said I was out of line, that my anger wasn't in the spirit of the game.

Bull. The problem with too many of these so-called oldtimers games is that the promoters—and sometimes the players themselves—have a tendency to clown around, knowing that no one's in shape. They end up ridiculing themselves, and that really bothers me. I never want to see great athletes ridiculed! If you want to see clowns, go watch the Globetrotters. I have too much respect for men who played in the professional ranks to ever sit back and laugh at them when they can't get the job done anymore.

That's what it all comes down to, in my mind anyway: A matter of respect. That's always been important to me.

I guess I have what you'd call a competitive streak. It's always been there. It still is, whether I'm trying to solve a puzzle, or maybe proving to myself that I can still climb stairs *two* at a time. Maybe it's playing racquetball singles when I know I should cut down. That's a mistake, but it's one I can't help making.

Ever since I was a little kid I've always set goals. I wanted to be the best athlete in elementary school, P.S. 122, and I worked hard to become, if not the best, one of the best. I've always had the idea that if I was going to try to do something, it made no sense at all to give it less than my best shot.

Tenacity of purpose! That's the phrase I like to use.

By the time I got to college I was a pretty good scorer. I wasn't a real strong guy, but I knew the game. Most of all I was smart, especially on defense. I was a lot like KC Jones—not as good as he was, of course—but a tenacious defensive player who could bother the hell out of the guy he was guarding.

The result was, I got into several fights when I first joined the team at George Washington. I think I had two or three my first week there. They had a lot of great players from the New York area—Silkowitz, Garber, O'Brien, Aronson, Karp—plus some who were all-state from places like Indiana and Oregon: Osborne, Faris, Butterworth. Here I was, a transfer from a junior college, joining guys who'd had a great year the season before, and I wanted to play!

Day after day, I belted heads with these guys, but Osborne, Karp, Aronson and Garber were all guards, just like me. How the hell was I supposed to break in?

The answer was defense. I was all over them like a blanket, hounding them every step, shutting them off every chance I got. Naturally, they didn't like it, so one thing led to another and before you knew it, fists were flying.

The same thing happened when I showed up at Norfolk Naval Station after college. They had a great basketball team there—Holzman, Zunic, Feerick; like Jim Floyd of Oklahoma A&M and Earl Keth of Missouri; major league baseball players like Charlie Wagner from Boston, Johnny Rigney, and Phil Rizzuto.

At that time, around 1943, Norfolk Naval Station, Norfolk Air Station, and the military base at Great Lakes probably had the three best basketball teams in the country.

So we had a practice one day, and I was assigned to guard Floyd, the captain. I held him scoreless and he got steamed. Maybe he had a right to get mad. I hadn't played for a while, so probably I was grabbing him more than I should have.

"What's the matter?" I asked him. "Can't you take it? Somebody plays a little defense against you and you don't know what the hell to do."

That was it. We start slugging it out.

Looking back, I can see how playing against a guy like me might be infuriating. No one played that kind of defense back then. As a result your offenses weren't set up to include screens, picks and special plays designed to get a man free. That meant a guy like me could easily become a real pain in the neck to someone who was accustomed to shooting the ball without a lot of aggravation.

That was my style. That was my intent. I was always looking for that extra edge, and what better edge could you get than to have the man you were guarding lose his composure?

I remember when Paul Silas joined us in Boston. I was coming into my late 50s at the time, and he'd heard a lot about my competitiveness on the tennis court, about the way I reacted to challenges. So we got to kidding about it, and I finally said: "Okay, let's go. You and me. One on one."

It was after practice in the gym and everyone gathered to watch. Talk about a knock-down-drag-out affair! I knew he didn't have an outside shot and I wasn't going to let him get around me; so I figured I had a chance. He'd shoot, I'd shove him, grab the ball and head down the court. The score got to 6–6, and you needed 7 to win.

Now everyone's up, yelling, and we're really getting into it. I get the ball, fake him, he pushes me, and I finally get the shot off—but it hits the backboard; I miss.

His ball. I'm belting him all the way down the floor—I mean, there's blood up and down the line! —and now he takes me into the pivot.

"Hey, goddamn it," I tell him. "If you hurt me, I can't sign your checks."

That was my little edge, right? Made no difference. He's too hot to care. We fight a little bit longer, then finally he lays in the winning shot. But he *knew* he'd been in a game; he really did.

It's all over and we're standing there sweating, looking at each other.

"Damn!" he said, laughing. "You *never* quit. No wonder you guys won all those flags."

That made me feel pretty good.

But it was also the last time I ever played one-on-one in a serious vein.

Am I what they say I am? Am I *who* they say I am? Who can answer questions like that? They aren't fair questions. I'll say this, however: I was never a faker. I never considered myself a sham. To the best of my ability I was always an upfront guy. As I mentioned earlier, if there's one part of my father that I'd like to think people can see in me today, it would be his integrity.

My guys knew that if I told them something, they could rely on it. To me, that was one of the most important assets I had. I would back up anything I told a player. I had to if I wanted to earn his respect. If the players believed my word was no good, then I'd have been gonzo in their eyes.

Maybe that's the thing which pleases me most when I hear old Celtics talking about their coach. My word was good. And to whatever extent it was possible, all of my actions were directed toward one goal, and that was to make the Celtics the best damn team in the world.

You hear a lot of talk about the "American Dream." In a way I suppose I'm an example of it. I certainly didn't inherit my money. But what I have is *more* than money. I mean, I never worried about becoming a millionaire. That was never important to me. If it had been, I'd have fought for a piece of the team every time the Celtics were sold, which was often.

Some sons of immigrants turn out to be very wealthy people and they think *that's* the solution. That's what makes them Horatio Algers: They start with a little store and build it into a great chain, or whatever.

Well, I don't agree. They're just guys who made it big in business. To me, it's more than money. Money's only part of the dream. The dream is to be whatever you set out to be, to accomplish all of your goals, to fulfill your own potential.

I always thought my biggest forte was teaching. I'd have made a good college professor. Want to know what one of my biggest thrills was? I'll tell you.

Back when I was teaching in high school I developed what I liked to call my Potential Limit Theory. Basically, it came down to this: Everyone is born with a certain potential. You will never achieve your full potential, but how close you come depends on how much you want to pay the price—and, if you're in sports, the type of coaching you receive, things like that.

Let's say a man's born to jump 20 feet. On his own, maybe he'll jump 15 feet. He's called a natural athlete. But with proper guidance and hard work, he might get up to 19 feet; it's unlikely he'll ever hit 20. Someone else might have a potential limit of 15 feet. With 10 times the amount of dedication that the first guy has, the best he'll ever do is 14 feet. The natural athlete will beat him every time.

To me, the tragedy of sports is that so many kids who are born with great natural talent, great natural ability, never come close to realizing their full potential, either because of poor coaching or their inability to absorb good coaching, or, more often, their unwillingness to pay the price. All this wonderful promise goes by the boards.

Many, many times, the kids with less talent become the better athletes because they're more dedicated to achieving their fullest potential. At least, that's how the theory goes.

So one day I'm walking down a street in New York and this fellow stops me.

"You don't remember me . . ."

It was S. Lee Pogostin. He'd been a student of mine—just fair; B, maybe—and he played some ball, but not well enough to make the team. He wasn't the kind of kid you took much notice of, but now he'd become a pretty well-known writer; he'd adapted *The Moon and Sixpence* for television, and things like that.

"You know," he said, "you taught me something in one of my classes that I've never forgotten."

"What was that?" I asked.

"You once gave a lecture on the theory of Potential Limit . . ."

Man, I was sky-high the rest of the day.

But getting back to the business of the American Dream, have I lived it? Am I living it? Yes. No question about it. But ask me if I've achieved my own potential limit, and the answer obviously is no.

This is my 39th season in the league. Obviously, then, my potential limit would have been to win 39 championships. But we've won only 15.

When you look at it that way, I haven't even come close.

2.

My Kind of Guys

"The fun part of basketball is winning."

Whenever I hear someone talking about a Celtic-type player it makes me feel good, because I like to think we've come to represent more than just banners and rings, although they're important, too: They symbolize the truth of what we've been preaching down through the years.

The Celtics represent a philosophy which, in its simplest form, maintains that the victory belongs to the team. Individual honors are nice, but no Celtic has ever gone out of his way to achieve them. We've never had the league's top scorer. In fact, we won seven championships without placing even one Celtic among the league's Top 10. But on twelve of our championship teams we had six (and, on four occasions, *seven*) players averaging in double figures.

Our pride was never rooted in statistics. Our pride was in our identity as the Boston Celtics. Being a Celtic meant you were someone special, because everyone knew the Celtics played smart, exciting, championship basketball. But this all starts with getting the right kind of players.

My kind of kid had the ability to absorb coaching. He was a kid who'd react to whatever I told him. He was a nice kid on and off the court, not someone who'd be bitching all the time. Some kids become real pains in the ass once they get a taste of stardom. I wanted a kid who was great, yet never stopped being nice. Most of all, I wanted a kid who was willing to pay the price, willing to work at winning. I wanted a kid who wanted to win so bad that he wouldn't think twice about giving me everything he had. That was a Celtic-type player in my eyes. That was Frank Ramsey. That was John Havlicek. That's Larry Bird. But that was also a lot of other great players who never received the loud ovations, who never got the headline stories, but who nevertheless were vitally instrumental to our success. KC Jones, Satch Sanders, Don Chaney: they're my kind of guys, too.

We were the first organization to popularize the concept of the "role player," the player who willingly undertakes the thankless job that has to be done in order to make the whole package fly.

When I talk about role players, I'm not talking about the Sixth Man, and I'll tell you why. The Sixth Man role is something else altogether. We invented it back in 1957 with Ramsey; then Havlicek took it over when Frank retired in 1964. Paul Silas inherited it when he joined us in 1972, and he helped win two championships with the boosts he gave us coming off the bench. Today, Kevin McHale wears that hat, and it fits him just as comfortably as it fit the others.

The average player's ego tells him he must be in the starting five if he wants to feel important. But my "starting five" weren't necessarily the five players on the court when the game began; it was the guys on the floor at the end of the game who mattered most to me, because that's when you need your coolest heads and surest hands. Most teams start their five best players. But I stopped doing that. I began starting 80 percent of my best. What happened then?

After five, six or seven minutes, everyone on the court starts getting a bit weary. That's when the substitutions start. So while the opposition *decreased* its efficiency by bringing in a lesser talent, I *increased* ours by bringing in a Ramsey who'd either maintain the tempo we had begun or else turn it up a notch. Psychologically, this was very damaging to opponents who, instead of getting a breather, found they had to work even harder to keep up with us.

Far from being unsung, the Sixth Man became a prestigious assignment in Boston. But when you talk about "role players," that's something different.

When you ask a man to play a role, it doesn't mean he lacks the skills to shoot, or that he couldn't fit into the flow of your attack as well as anyone else. It just means that someone has to be designated to guard the toughest player on the other side, to sacrifice himself for the good of his own club.

I made sure that players who filled those roles on our teams were adequately compensated, because their contributions to winning were as important as anyone else's. People seem to have the idea that if a man isn't putting points on the board it means he's a second-rate member of the cast. That's ridiculous—almost as ridiculous as the general perception that if you're not scoring points, you're not having fun.

The fun part of basketball isn't shooting. The fun part of basketball is winning. That's what's fun. *Winning!* I don't care what your "role" is, when your team's winning and you know you're a part of it, that's happiness.

Playing "roles," which simply means playing to your individual strengths, not only makes sense for the ballclub; it makes sense for the players, too, if they stop to think about it.

Take Don Nelson. The Lakers placed him on waivers in 1965. That's how we acquired him, after everyone else had a shot at him and turned thumbs down. He was resigned to the fact that his career was over—until we picked him up and showed him how he could fit into the Celtics' scheme of things. He ended up playing eleven seasons in Boston, and when he was done we retired his number. Today he owns five championship rings.

What did we do with him? We used his smarts, his ability to shoot after one or two fakes, his skills at boxing out. If we had just turned him loose and allowed him to float in the general swing of things—hey, that's why LA let him go! He wasn't productive that way.

Look at a guy like Jim Loscutoff. He played nine years with us. He was our "cop" after Bob Brannum retired, but that wasn't enough to keep him in the league so long. Loscy made it on his defense, his boxing out, his ability to set great screens. If I had told him, "Don't worry about all that other stuff; just get us some points," he might have lifted his average a little bit, but the other parts of his game would have suffered so much that we'd have had to let him go.

Take Satch Sanders. With great shooters like Tommy Heinsohn, Bill Sharman, Bob Cousy, Frank Ramsey, John Havlicek and Sam Jones around, I didn't need any points from Satch, just like I didn't need much from Russell. Sure, I wanted him to take the shot if the other team insulted him by giving him too much room, but what I really wanted from him was outstanding D, strong, tough, relentless pressure on people like Elgin Baylor who'd kill you if you left them alone.

Satch tells a great story on himself which sheds a lot of light on how we felt as a team.

There was a time around his third or fourth year with us when he got to thinking that it might be nice to score a few points of his own. So without being too obvious about it, he began taking more shots. One night he scored 15 points. Another night he managed to get 18. Meanwhile, no one said a word about it. Our policy was that the ball belonged to everyone; nobody had exclusive rights to it. If you thought you had a good shot, you were not only encouraged to take it, you were *expected* to take it.

Then one night he scored around 20 points, and we lost. It bothered him all the way home. He thought about it long into the night, then came to the following conclusion: "All it takes to upset the balance of this beautiful machine of ours is one man crossing over into another man's specialty. So I decided that night that it was a much bigger claim to say that I was a member of the world champions than it was to say I averaged 35 points a game. Once I realized that, I never worried about scoring again."

Talk about a winning attitude! Satch epitomized the way we played the game in Boston.

The most overdone aspect of sports is statistics, and baseball's the worst offender of all. *What's his batting average?* That's the big concern. Hell, one guy might go a month in which he'll get 10 hits off the end of his bat: scratch singles, little windblown pops that just fall in at the edge of the grass. Meanwhile, the rest of his game is strictly for the birds. There's another guy, however, who's belting the ball all over the place—line drives to all fields, ropes which the third baseman stabs—but none of the breaks are going his way. If his luck just turned around, he'd be twice the player the other guy is. Yet at contract time he's hitting .240 and the other fellow's hitting .280, so he gets $150,000 while the guy with the banjo winds up making half a million.

The bottom line should never be numbers. The bottom line should be winning. The bottom line should take into account a player's overall contributions to success, especially his attitude. If I'd been a baseball man, my kind of guys would have been people like Eddie Stanky, people like Billy Martin, people who were invaluable when it came to pepping up other players, to keeping everyone on his toes; people whose only goal was to win and to play as a team unit.

And if I was a football man, I'd have wanted a Jim Plunkett. Maybe his average wouldn't compare with some of those guys who keep firing their three-yard passes. They'll complete eight out of ten, but they're going nowhere. I'll take Plunkett's three out of ten, because two of them are going to bring us down the field and put us into position to score.

If we had gone strictly by stats we never would have kept a KC Jones. We never would have kept a Sanders. We wouldn't have kept a Chaney. Yet if those three never scored one single point for us, we still would have considered them brilliant stars because they cost our opposition *thousands* of points.

So what do numbers mean? Back in the early '50s we had a guy named Bob Donham who had a field goal percentage of .507 as a rookie, .480 overall, yet he couldn't hit the side of a barn. He was the worst shooter we had, but Cousy kept hitting him with beautiful passes at the end of the break, so his numbers were phenomenal.

I'll never forget the night we were playing at Philadelphia—this was back in the old days, before Russell—and it all came down to one shot. I don't remember what play we set up, but I know it didn't work because Donham ended up with the ball. He was 25 feet from the basket, which meant he'd have been lucky to hit the backboard. But time was running out and he had no choice, so he stepped back and let it fly—and *swish!* we win.

Eddie Gottlieb, the Philadelphia owner, caught up with me after the game, and he still couldn't believe what happened.

"God, Red," he kept saying. "Donham! I would have expected the ballboy to shoot before you'd let Donham have it at a moment like that."

"Eddie," I said, "What can I tell you? We're in a funny business."

When you talk about character, you're talking about the clutch shot, the last-second shot that's going to decide whether you go home a winner or a loser.

Take my word for it, there have been many great stars in the NBA who avoided that shot like a plague. They just didn't want the responsibility of possibly failing when all eyes were on them.

But we never considered it failure to miss a shot at a moment like that. I never, ever bawled out a player of mine for missing the clutch shot. I'd tell him: "Hey, you tried your best and the ball wouldn't drop. That's life."

If, however, we failed to execute well enough to at least attempt a good shot, that was a different matter. That's when I'd get mad. I'd get mad at the guy who blew the play, who failed to set the right screen. Or I'd get mad at the guy who had the good shot and wouldn't take it. But to take a good shot and miss it? Hell, that could happen to anyone.

We always had guys who *wanted*—who *welcomed*—the responsibility of taking the final shot. The challenge excited them. The pressure just aroused their pride. *"Hey, give me the ball. I'll shoot the damned thing up there, and I'll live with the consequences."*

Bob Cousy. Frank Ramsey. Tommy Heinsohn. Sam Jones. John Havlicek. They loved being forced to rise to any occasion. That's when they were at their best. In the tightest of situations, when many so-called stars looked for ways to retreat, these guys came on like gangbusters.

Even Russell merits a mention here. Sure, everyone knew what he would do at *his* end of the court in a spot like that. You knew he'd make the big defensive play, or block the shot, or grab the rebound. But offensively he was just as tough in the clutch. He'd blow free throws all night long, but if the game hung in the balance when he stepped up to the line, he'd drop those shots right into the hole. That's character. And Bird's just the latest in a long line of Celtics who embody the word.

I've never liked going into names, except in specific situations, when it comes to handing out praise, because to single out a few is to disregard the contributions of so many others. That's especially true when it comes to the Celtics: Our whole philosophy is that *every* member is important; *every* role is vital.

I think of a guy like Gabby Harris, a forward we had in the early '50s: Limited talent, no question about it. Yet every night he gave us everything he possessed.

Same with Bob Brannum, our policeman back then,

a real muscle guy. I admired him as much as any player I ever had, because I always knew we could count on him for every ounce of ability he possessed.

Then there was a guy like Ed Macauley. He gets a big laugh nowadays by saying he's the most valuable player we ever had because he's the guy we "got rid of" in order to acquire Russell. It's a good line, but you'd never catch me laughing. And if anyone else ever said that in my presence I'd knock him off his feet.

I had a lot of fondness for Macauley. He worked so hard, and he was an outstanding leader, but his body was so light and frail that by playoff time guys would just look at him and he'd fall over. It wasn't his fault; he'd exhausted himself all winter long.

I was always after him to eat a hearty pregame meal. So one time we had an important playoff game scheduled for a Friday night, and I told him to be sure he loaded up. But he was a devout Catholic, a very religious person. "Red," he told me, "I can't eat meat today."

My mind started conjuring up images of him running out of gas in the first quarter.

"What about the dispensation business?" I asked him. "Can't you get a special dispensation? We've got to win this one."

"Well, yes . . . I suppose it's possible," he said.

So the two of us turned the railroad station upside down looking for a priest. We finally located one who gave Ed permission to eat a decent meal. I thanked him very much, then took my center across the street and bought him a big plate of lamb chops.

It's always bothered me that Sam Jones is overshadowed in the public mind by Cousy, Russell and Havlicek—even though he's in the Hall of Fame, and even though he was voted onto the NBA's Silver Anniversary all-star team.

Sam's one of the few people who can claim to have left an indelible mark on the game.

Hank Luisetti introduced the one-hand shot. George Mikan introduced the hook. Wilt Chamberlain popu-

larized the dunk. Kareem Abdul-Jabbar made the sky
hook famous; Bobby Davies was the creator of the
behind-the-back dribble, which Bob Cousy then popu-
larized; and Oscar Robertson was the model for the
modern do-it-all guard.

Sam had his trademark, too: The use of the backboard to bank in that soft jump shot from the side.
Before Sam turned it into an art, very few people even
knew how to shoot a bank shot; 70 percent of your
designated scorers tried to aim the ball straight in, and
those who did attempt to use the backboard had no
clear idea of what they were doing.

But when Sam took that shot, it was money in the
bank, no pun intended. Next to an uncontested dunk,
Sam's bank shot might have been the surest two points
in the league. And he was just as deadly under pressure, maybe even more so, because his concentration
was increased.

Watch Dr. J today. Whenever he's at the side of
the lane, he kisses that ball off the backboard. Watch a
kid like Mike Mitchell. Same thing. Watch hundreds of
kids in hundreds of gyms all across the country today.
They're all banking in soft jumpers.

That's the mark Sam Jones left on the game. It's
his shot they're shooting, but none of them will ever
shoot it any better than he did. He was the best.

Tommy Heinsohn is another guy who never gets
the credit he deserves. Everyone thought he was a
shooter. They called him "Gunner."

Well, it's true. He *was* a shooter, but that's what I
wanted him to be. I told him to shoot. That was his job,
and he was damned good at it. But people forget he
also could pass, and he was one of the best offensive
rebounders of his time.

He was one of my "whipping boys." The other was
Loscutoff. Whenever I had a point I wanted the whole
team to hear, they were the guys I'd yell at. Their hides
were thick; they could take it. Other players might have
gotten angry or embarrassed. Not these two. In one ear
and out the other. I don't think they even heard half

the things I said, which was all right with me. It was the rest of the team I was directing the message to.

One night we ran up a 25- or 30-point halftime lead. It was no contest. So I walked into our dressing room, and as soon as the door closed behind me, Heinsohn jumped up. "Okay, Red," he said, "I didn't rebound, I didn't block out, I didn't shoot. What else didn't I do?"

Everyone started to laugh. Me, too. What could I say?

Tommy was tough, tougher than most people realize, because he also happens to be a very warm, outgoing guy who likes people and has a great sense of humor.

I'll always remember the night I asked him to play a special "role." We were up against Philadelphia in the playoffs, which meant having to contend with Wilt. So I devised a play that called for Tommy to stand in Wilt's path whenever he started to chase after Russell. Wilt had to be one of the strongest men in the world, and when he finally caught on to what Tommy was doing, he got madder than hell and ran right up Heinsohn's back a couple of times. But Heinie never budged and never complained. He just stood his ground and continued doing the job all night long. That's why I loved the guy.

He also coached us to two championships, in 1974 and 1976, after taking the job when Russell retired.

They were all Celtic-type players. It's a hard thing to define. It's an attitude, really. Sometimes I think it shows up most in players who started their careers somewhere else and then wound up in Boston. Willie Naulls. Paul Silas. Wayne Embry. Charlie Scott. Dennis Johnson. The list goes on. Ask any of them, and they'll all tell you that what impressed them most upon joining the Celtics was that now they were part of a unit, part of a family whose only purpose was to win as a team.

Dave Cowens might have been the most emotional Celtic of all. He played with an incredible level of intensity; it was almost as if you could see the sparks in his eyes once he made up his mind to do something.

We got him in the 1970 draft, one year after Russell retired. We were in urgent need of a starting center and we had the fourth overall pick that spring, the highest Celtic pick since 1950. There was a good crop of big men coming out this year: Bob Lanier, Sam Lacey, Bobby Croft, Dan Issel. Those were the names everyone was talking about.

No one knew much about Cowens, except that, at 6-8½, he didn't seem to have the size to become a great NBA center. His school, Florida State, was prohibited from playing in the NCAA tournament because of recruiting violations, so that kept him out of the national limelight. But I'd heard enough about him to intrigue me; so I went down to take a look in person, and I couldn't believe my eyes. In fact, he was so good it scared me. I got up and left in the third quarter, trying my best not to show my excitement, hoping no one else in the league knew what I learned that night.

As soon as I got back to Boston I told Heinsohn: "Tommy, I've found your center."

All that remained was sweating out the draft. Lanier went first. Then San Diego took Rudy Tomjanovich, and Atlanta selected Pete Maravich.

We had him!

Russell went down to Florida to meet him, and when he came back he was as impressed as I had been. "Red," he told me, "you've got a great one there."

"What makes you so sure?" I asked him. "You've never even seen him play."

"I talked with him," he said, "and I looked into his eyes. Believe me, I *know*. This kid's going to be something."

Cowens became one of the great competitors of all time. He didn't just play the game, he *attacked* it.

I think my favorite Cowens story is the night he fouled Mike Newlin. It's a classic.

We were playing Houston, and Dave was sky high, as usual. He set a pick, then turned to face the basket—and Calvin Murphy went sprawling onto the floor. Dave had just nudged him; hell, since Murphy was only 5-9, he probably didn't even see him. It was an act, but they called a foul—and right away you could see the frustration on his face.

The next thing you know, Newlin took a dive. Another foul on Cowens. Now Dave was livid. He was a banger, a scrapper; he just wanted to play. This penny-ante foolishness was eating him up. I knew something was going to happen; that fire came into his eyes.

Play resumes and he starts running downcourt, and then he spots Newlin. Poor Newlin never knew what hit him. Dave plowed into him like a freight train, knocking him through the air about 12 feet. Then, without even waiting for Newlin to land, he turned to the officials and, in a voice loud enough for the whole crowd to hear, he yelled: "Now *that's* a foul!" That was Cowens.

Then one day in November 1976 he came to me, five months after he'd led us to his second championship in three seasons, and told me he was fed up with basketball, exhausted, and just couldn't do it anymore. He wanted to quit. He was 28.

"Dave," I told him, "if you don't want to play anymore, there's nothing I can do. That's life."

Sure, I could have ranted and raved: What about your teammates? What about your fans? What about your obligations to all these people? But I couldn't do that to him. I had too much respect for the guy, and I could see he was emotionally wiped out. If a guy's that unhappy, you can't force him into a better mood. All you'll do is worsen his attitude.

He wanted to quit for an indefinite period. If I had pushed him at that moment, maybe he'd have quit for good. Who knows? But that's what was running through my mind.

"Keep in touch," I said. "We'll talk. And when you think you're ready to come back, when you've regained your peace of mind, we'll go at 'em again, okay?" That's how we left it.

He took quite a beating in some of the papers and on most of the talk shows; there was very little sympathy for his position. People said he was a flake. They insinuated he was selfish and disloyal. They made it sound like he was a soldier going AWOL or a sailor jumping ship. The abuse he took was mean, cutting and undeserved.

That was the other reason I made no attempt to argue with him when he told me how he felt. He displayed the highest ethics in that situation that anyone could possibly imagine. He could have been cute about it. He could have said, "My back hurts; I can't play." No one would have criticized that, and he could have continued cashing his paychecks. Believe me, it's been done before.

But that's not Cowens. This kid's too principled for that. "Look," he said that day, "I'm not injured. There's nothing wrong with me, so I don't want to be paid. I just don't feel like playing anymore." How could I argue with that?

You see, an athlete's not a piece of meat. He's a person. And people get fed up with things. That's why Russell quit; the fires went out. He just stopped caring, and he couldn't play that way, so rather than hang around an extra few years like a mercenary, he walked away with his pride intact. Havlicek was different. John was the most even-tempered kid I ever coached; he had the perfect temperament for an athlete. But he started getting grouchy at the end; things that never bothered him before were starting to get under his skin. That's what told him it was time to get out. With that body of his, he could have played five more years. But he was smart enough to know that once the enjoyment goes out the window, there's nothing left to play for.

That's how Cowens felt, and unlike Bill or John, he couldn't have altered his tempo and picked his spots. There was only one gear to Dave's game: Full speed ahead.

Suppose I had convinced him to keep on playing and he suffered a nervous breakdown? I'd have been the cause of it.

In my mind, he was an injured player. He was

emotionally injured: Injuries don't have to be physical. You can be injured in spirit. That's what was wrong with him. I appreciated his problem, I respected his integrity, and I wished him nothing but the best as he walked out my door.

He came back later that season after missing 30 games and spent the next three years with us. They included the two worst years of my entire association with the Celtics, 1977–78 and 1978–79, a horrible period of ownership problems and personnel turnovers in which we lost 103 games. Havlicek retired in the middle of that stretch, and for a while Dave tried his hand as a player-coach. We didn't see daylight again until the spring of 1979, when the ownership mess was finally resolved and Larry Bird was on his way.

Cowens and Bird—what a pair they'd have made when Dave was in his prime—had one season together, then Dave called it quits. Now it was physical injuries that were bogging him down. He was 32, and his body just couldn't take the beating it was getting every game.

He walked onto the team bus in the middle of training camp, 1980, and told his teammates goodby. Seven months later we were champions again. I wish he could have shared in that.

He stayed away from the game for two years. Then he started to feel good again, so he came to me in the summer of '82 and said he wanted to give it one last go—but not in Boston. There were several reasons for that. One was that his good friend, Don Nelson, was now coaching in Milwaukee. Another was that he felt fans' expectations there wouldn't be unrealistic, that no one in Milwaukee would be comparing him to what he had been back in the days of his youth. The young Dave Cowens was gone forever, and he knew that better than anyone.

So I went along with him, working out a deal with the Bucks that brought Quinn Buckner to Boston and allowed Dave to suit up in Milwaukee. But just before he left I had a little talk with him.

"Dave," I told him, "there's only one way you can play this game, and if your body can't take it, then it's not going to work. You can't play a pussyfoot game. That's not you."

And it was true. He never could have been a back-court-type player, a perimeter guy. He was like Bobby Orr in hockey: he had to be where the action was. Orr quit when his body wouldn't allow him to play his game. And that's what happened to Dave. He played 40 games with the Bucks, and then hung them up for good.

But that was just a footnote to a truly spectacular career. He was always a Celtic at heart, and he'll always be one of my favorites. No one ever played to win more than that guy did.

Nothing could get me more irritated than watching an athlete fail to realize his own potential. I never asked anyone to be great. I just said: "Be as good as you can be! You owe it to yourself, you owe it to me and you owe it to the team."

Take the simple skill of shooting a basketball. You're born with a certain ability to coordinate your eyes with your muscles; your eyes see something and your muscles react. I'll take a ball, hand it to someone, and tell him to throw it into that barrel over there. He might do it 18 out of 20 attempts. The guy standing next to him might do it just eight times out of 20. Why? Their eyes are different; the weight of the object affects them differently; their releases are different.

I can tell the first guy: "Look, turn your wrists this way, instead of following through so much . . . " I can improve his style; I can adjust his rhythm. I can help him become a better shooter.

The other guy? Maybe I can help him get to a point where he shoots the ball into the barrel 14 times—but he'll never do better than that.

It's like a Don Chaney or a KC Jones. No matter how much we worked with them or how much they tried—and both had tremendous willingness to learn—there was no way in the world we could have made them shoot like Bill Sharman or Sam Jones. It simply wasn't there. Some things can't be taught. You can't teach a passer to have Bob Cousy's peripheral vision.

So what you do, in cases like that, is find another phase of the player's game to work on, some strong point which can be developed into an important skill. Quite often it's defense. See, defense *can* be taught, because it's largely a matter of hard work, concentration, and balance. It's more than a matter of touch. Sometimes it's as simple as telling yourself: "If I can't get that rebound, *he's* not going to get it either." Bang. You hit him, bump him, whatever. There are a lot of techniques you can develop once you put your mind to it.

Offense is different. Offense *is* touch. It's something you're born with. And there's no explaining why some guys have it and some guys don't. I've seen great pure shooters: Bill Sharman, Sam Jones, Rick Barry, Austin Carr, Oscar Robertson; I could name 20 others. I've also seen wonderful shooters who broke every rule in the book, whose form was so bad you hoped no kids were watching, yet they managed to put the ball into the hole, which was all that mattered. Tommy Heinsohn was like that. So was Frank Ramsey. So were guys like Bob Feerick and Freddy Scolari from the old days.

People like them I left alone. Why tinker with success?

Remember what I said before about a player's potential limit? I think that's what these guys, these great Celtic-type players, had in common: They all got as much out of themselves as there was to get. The ideal situation, of course, is to find the athlete who has the innate ability, who has the right attitude, who has received the right kind of coaching, and who is willing to pay the price.

Larry Bird has come as close to reaching his potential limit as any athlete I've ever seen. He was born with great eye-hand coordination, but then he *learned* good form, learned to follow through and things like that, learned how to move closer and closer to whatever potential he had. Take anybody else with Bird's basic abilities and give him poor work habits, along with an inability to concentrate, and he'd be a hack.

Who might have had the greatest potential limit of all? That's hard to say. Probably Wilt Chamberlain. But Wilt got to a point very early in his career where he wasn't coachable anymore. He worked hard when he wanted to work hard, but he couldn't be pushed any more than he wanted to push himself, and usually he pushed himself in the direction of his own personal pride and his own personal achievements.

Whether I, or any other coach, might have changed him we'll never know. I tend to doubt it. He was a giant among giants, a great athlete; I'll never take that away from him. Yet he should have been so much better than he was. Not that he didn't want his team to win, mind you; I'd never accuse him of that. But he was much more interested in his own contributions than he was in the welfare of his team in general.

That's why Russell was better. Russell played with his head. He was better motivated. And most of all, he had the bigger heart.

This is what makes it difficult to judge most athletes' potential limit until you bring them onto your team. I didn't know what I was getting when I got Russell. I didn't know what I was getting when I got Bird. Sure, I knew enough about both of them to know that I'd do anything I could to put them into Celtic uniforms, but I had no way of knowing what surprises were laying in store for me. They weren't just great players; they were great Celtics.

3.

Russell or Bird?

"The hardest thing in the world for me to decide."

People are always asking me: *Who's the best player you ever saw?*

I tell them that's not a fair question. There are so many factors you have to consider: The era a man played in; the caliber of his teammates; the types of systems his coaches installed, and how well those systems were tailored to his particular skills. These are all important considerations.

A John Havlicek, for instance, would have been outstanding wherever he played. But a Bob Cousy? No way. He would not have been an outstanding player if he ended up someplace like Chicago in the kind of slowed-down game played when Dick Motta was there. Cousy would have been stifled; he needed a running game.

Quite often, the team makes the player—more often, in fact, than the player making the team, though it can work both ways. There's an old line about how the strength of the wolf is in the pack, and the strength of the pack is in the wolf; there's some truth on both sides. But though it's nice to have a guy who'll get you 35 points a game, that's not enough to win. Bernard King can score 55 points and the Knicks might still lose. It's happened. It used to happen all the time with Wilt Chamberlain. That year he averaged 50.4 with the old Philadelphia Warriors, we finished 11 games ahead of them.

But all factors being considered, if I *had* to pick the best of all, the answer would be easy.

Bill Russell and Larry Bird.

And I'm not picking them just because they're my guys; I'm calling them the best of all time because they *are* the best of all time.

Okay, you say, but there's a draft tomorrow—the hypothetical all-time draft—and I've got the first pick. Whose name do I call? That would be the hardest thing in the world for me to decide. I'll tell you why—and then I'll tell you whom I'd pick.

When Russell quit in 1969 I knew in my heart that we'd never see anything like him again, and no one's ever come along to change that opinion.

I'll be the first to admit I didn't know what we were getting when we drafted Bird. But people forget that it was the same thing when we drafted Bill. I knew we were acquiring someone who'd get us the ball. That was our big need back in '56, the one missing element that could make us a great, great team.

I'd heard about Russell when he was a sophomore at San Francisco. My old college coach, Bill Reinhart, had seen him play. He came back and told me, "Red, you've got two years. Start planning now. This kid can be outstanding." Reinhart was the first to spot it.

So, yes, getting him was premeditated. It was no accident. We wanted Russell. And we went after him, working out a deal with St. Louis in which we gave them Ed Macauley, who was our all-star center, and Cliff Hagan, who was just coming out of the Army and was certain to be a top-notch forward. In return, we got their first pick, which was the number two pick in the draft that year. Rochester had the first pick overall, but we already knew that they were taking Sihugo Green of Duquesne. We took Russell.

Did I know what I was getting? Not really. A great rebounder? Sure. But I knew nothing about his character, his smarts, his heart; things like that. You never know those things until you actually have the guy. No one in the league really thought much about it at the time. They certainly didn't know what was about to happen: 11 Boston championships in the next 13 years.

Most of your centers in those days—Mikan, Pettit, Johnston—were also your predominant scorers, and here was a guy who, word had it, couldn't hit the backboard; that wasn't really true, but that was the rap against him.

After we made the deal to get him, Walter Brown, our owner at the time, went with me to watch him perform in an exhibition game the Olympic team was playing at the University of Maryland. He was terrible. Just awful! Walter and I sat there looking at each other all night. What in the world had we done?

But later that night, after the game, Russell came over to see us. "I want to apologize," he said. "I am really embarrassed. That was the worst game I ever played."

So we talked about it, then got onto other things and it was never mentioned again. At the end of the night, after Russell left, Walter turned to me and asked, "Well, what do you think?"

"I was worried for a while," I told him. "But after looking into his eyes and hearing him talk like that, I'm not worried anymore."

Russ joined us in December 1956, after leading the Olympic team to a gold medal in Melbourne. I brought him into my office and we had a little talk.

"You're probably worried about scoring," I suggested, "because everyone says you don't shoot well enough to play ball."

"Well, yes," he smiled, "I am a little concerned about that."

"Okay," I told him. "I'll make a deal with you

today, right here and now. I promise that as long as you play here, whenever we talk about contracts we will *never* discuss statistics."

We never did. There was only one statistic that mattered to Russell, and it was the same one that mattered to me: Wins.

"Russ," I said, "we have a pretty good organization here. No cliques; everyone gets along real well. All we want you to do is something no one's ever been able to do for this team: Get us the ball. Forget everything else. Just get the ball."

He nodded and smiled again. "I can do that," he said.

A lot of great basketball minds didn't think he would make it, and if you analyzed their thinking, you could see their point. Take a guy like Walter Dukes. He was bigger than Russell, and he could shoot better. Why, then, was Russell so great while Dukes was just another player?

It was his ability to perform in the clutch. It was his brilliant mind. It was his great defensive anticipation, which led to his great ability to intimidate. And in addition to all of his innate abilities, Russell was a student of the game. Sure, he had quickness, reaction, all the tools he needed. But most of all, he was a thinker. If you faked him a certain way and wound up making a basket or grabbing a rebound, he'd file it away in his mind, and you'd never fool him the same way again.

We played the Knicks in one of his early games with us and Harry Gallatin ate him up. Harry knew his way around. He was cute. So the next time we played New York I started telling Russ: "You take so-and-so and I'll have Heinsohn take Gallatin." He didn't say anything at first, but then he pulled me aside just before the game started.

"I'd like to play Gallatin," he said. "It won't happen again."

I said okay, and as I watched him walking onto the court I knew that this was a momentous occasion. He *killed* Gallatin. See, his pride had been wounded, and that made Russell a dangerous man to deal with. It's like they say in the jungle: Don't ever wound a lion, or he'll be twice as deadly. When Russell's pride was hurt he became like that wounded lion, and God help anybody who got in his way.

I remember one day when I really got angry at him in practice. Russell hated practice. Everyone knew it, but none of us made a big deal about it because we knew the guy would give us 48 tough minutes every game. So I'd shut my eyes to the false hustle he was giving. Still, practice had its purpose, even for him, especially when we were working on plays. And sometimes I'd want him to put out just so he wouldn't upset the other players' timing. Those were the only times when I'd really get on him; otherwise, I'd allow him to set his own pace, figuring I didn't want him leaving all of his energy in a workout.

But one particular morning he was loafing more than usual, and pretty soon everyone else started goofing off, too. So I blew my whistle. "Okay," I said, "are we all done resting now? Good. Let's go! Let's have a twenty-minute scrimmage, real strong, and then we can all get out of here."

So they start in, but pretty soon they're loafing again. Now I blow my whistle and I'm steamed. "Out! Everybody out. Right now. Don't let me hear another ball bounce. Just get out."

They all scrammed, wondering what I was going to do next. But I wasn't going to do anything. The feeling just wasn't there that day, that's all. It happens sometimes. You have to know when to push and when to back off.

Now comes our next practice. "Listen up," I tell them. "We will not discuss what happened before. All I want is a good, hard practice today. Let's go."

Sure enough, Russell starts in loafing again. All he's giving me is more false hustle. I stop the practice.

"Damn it, Russell," I yelled. "You destroyed practice the other day, but you're not going to destroy this one. I'm going to go up into those stands, light a cigar, and I'm going to sit there two hours, three hours, four hours—whatever it takes—until I see a good 20-minute scrimmage. I don't care if you're here all day long. I'm going to see a workout, so make up your mind to that now."

I grabbed some cigars, went into the stands and blew the whistle for them to start.

They began to play, and after five minutes I started to laugh. I couldn't help it. Russell must have blocked 9,000 shots. He'd grab a rebound, throw the outlet pass, race downcourt to stuff in a shot, then beat everybody back on defense, where he wouldn't allow anyone to get within 18 feet of the basket. I watched this incredible display and thought to myself, "If I don't stop this right now, he's going to leave his next game right here in the Cambridge Y."

I decided the only way to handle it was to make a joke of it, so I blew my whistle and walked back onto the court.

"Russell," I said, "what the hell am I going to do with you? I didn't mean for you to play *that* good. Can't you give me a happy medium!"

Bill's calling card, his specialty, was the blocked shot. I began to notice that he didn't block shots the way all the other big guys blocked them. Chamberlain and all those other guys were what I called shot-swatters—seven-foot fly-swatters—who'd knock the ball out of bounds, or else belt it into the open court where anybody could retrieve it.

Russell didn't do that. With his great timing and body control, he'd hit the bottom of the ball, forcing it to pop up into the air like a rebound, which he'd then grab. Or else he'd redirect it into the hands of one of his teammates. Either way, we ended up with possession. He turned shot-blocking into an art, and he's the only man I've ever seen who could do that on a consistent basis. No one's ever been able to duplicate his style, although Bill Walton came the closest when he was healthy.

Russell took that one great skill and revolutionized the game by terrorizing the league. As word spread and his reputation grew, he began instilling fear into the hearts of all the great shooters. He didn't react the way other centers reacted, so these shooters never knew how to react to him. Most shot-blockers, anticipating a shot, would go into the air with the shooters. Not Russell. He was so quick, so fast, that he wouldn't make his move until after the ball had left the shooter's hand. Against other centers, they'd just go behind a screen, or fake, or maybe double pump. That didn't work with Russell. He'd just stand there, watching you, waiting for you to commit yourself. The moment you released the ball, he'd be on it like a cat.

Shooters would come racing down the court, stop, and go up for a jumper—but hesitate just long enough to ask themselves, *"Where is he?"* And that split-second was all it took for one of our other guys to catch up to them. In situations like those, which we saw all the time, Russell didn't have to move an inch to break up a play. His presence alone was so unnerving that opposing players would blow their shots just worrying about what he *might* do.

I used to lead teams of NBA stars on State Department tours all over the world. One summer our tour took us to Yugoslavia. When we offered to put on clinics, as we did wherever we went, the officials there told us they weren't interested. Apparently some AAU team had been there before us and was beaten easily by the Yugoslavian national team.

We tried to explain that there was a big difference in our country between pros and amateurs, but they didn't want to hear anything about it. All they knew was that the guys they had whipped had worn USA on their jerseys. There was nothing they wanted to learn from us, they said, and they were pretty arrogant about it.

That irritated me. I wanted to set the record straight, to show the fans over there that they hadn't seen the best America could offer, because of course that's never explained to them whenever poorly-trained pickup teams of American kids get their asses handed to them by pros behind the Iron Curtain.

Yugoslavia had this redheaded center who was the leading scorer in all of Europe. So I pulled Russell aside just before the game got under way. "Look," I told him, "don't worry about the ball tonight. Don't worry about rebounds. Let Pettit and Heinsohn worry about that stuff. All I want you to do is guard that big kid over there. If he scores one basket, I'm going to break your neck. Understand?"

We start the game and the kid gets the ball. He fakes right, bounces once to his left, then goes up into the air—and you can see this big smile on his face. All of a sudden, Russell uncoils his arm. Blocked shot. We take the ball to the other end of the court and score.

This happened again. And again. And again. Russell blocked about six shots in a row, and now the kid's going bananas. He comes down the court a seventh time, takes two steps backward and throws the ball like a baseball.

"Damn it, Russell," I yell, "you let him hit the backboard!"

Russ looks at me. Now he's figuring he's got to find a way to get both the kid and me off his back. So the next time the guy takes a shot, instead of blocking it again he smacked it as hard as he could and it hit the kid in the face. He began screaming, going into a tantrum like a three-year-old, and he winds up kicking the ball into the crowd.

That was it for him. Technical foul. They threw him out of the game—the hero of the country, mind you. He had seen all he wanted to see.

That's what Russell could do when he put his mind to it.

Would we have had the success we enjoyed without Bill Russell? No way. But would he have had the same success if he played for another coach? I don't know.

I do know this. When I let it be known at the start of the 1965–66 season that I was beginning my final year of coaching, he came to me, more than once, and urged me not to quit. He called my wife and urged her not to let me quit.

Then one day late in that season, when he realized my mind was made up, he came to me and said he'd like to take over as coach when I retired. His reason was that he didn't want to play for anyone else. Suppose he didn't like the new guy? Or suppose the new guy brought in a different system after all these years?

Well, my mind started moving pretty fast. Suppose the new guy didn't understand Russell? Suppose they weren't able to develop a productive chemistry? I started thinking the same way Russell was thinking.

"I don't want to play for anybody else," he told me. "If I can't play for you, I'd rather play for myself, if you'll let me have the job."

I jumped at the idea. What better way to motivate Russell, I thought to myself, than to make him accountable for the whole team's performance? Remember, the year I left the bench we won our eighth championship in a row. Every season it became more difficult to sustain the intensity. But I knew Russell's pride, and if anybody could get the most out of Russell the player, it would be Russell the coach. Now there would be *two* reasons he had to win! Talk about a great self-motivating situation.

At our breakup banquet that spring, after all of the other speakers had been to the mike, Russ got up and talked about replacing me. He was leading up to a point, and when he got there he turned and looked directly at me.

"People say Red was lucky to have me," he said. "And he was. But I was lucky to have him, too. Red, you and I are going to be friends until one of us dies."

My throat got tight and my eyes filled and I had to look away. Lucky to have him? You bet I was.

I'm not much for showing my emotions in public, but I did that night.

I almost did it again when they had that big weekend for me in Boston. After all of my old players, from the '50s, '60s, '70s, right down to the present club, had assembled on the Garden court, they announced my name, and I walked out into the middle of a tremendous ovation. It was very emotional, but I was in full control as I started shaking hands with each old Celtic.

Then as I started moving toward Russell he held his arms out, and I stretched my arms, and the next thing I knew he was lifting me off the floor and holding me in a bear hug. Everyone was cheering, but all I was thinking was that I didn't want to cry because I was afraid I might not be able to stop. I almost cracked, but I got through it.

You see, what Russell and I share will always be special. My wife loves the guy. I love the guy. I understand him, just like he understands me. As he once said, we have the most essential ingredient for friendship, and that's mutual respect. He made no demands of me, and I made no demands of him. As he likes to say, we "exchanged favors."

One year, the night before training camp opened, I called him to my room. "Russ," I told him, "I'm going to yell at you all day long tomorrow. I may yell at you all week long. Don't pay any attention to it, okay? You see, if I can't yell at you, then I can't yell at anybody." He said that would be okay, so for the next couple of days I really climbed all over him, and he didn't react. I figured that was because of the little agreement we'd made. It wasn't until later that he told me I'd gotten him so mad he wanted to kill me. I was such a good actor that I guess I forgot I was acting.

Other times he'd come to me and ask if he could skip a practice, or maybe travel ahead by himself and meet the team on the road. It didn't happen often, but if I thought it really meant a lot to him I'd sometimes go along with his request. And I'd always add one condition: "You owe me one."

He'd laugh and say okay. Some night, maybe a month or two later, we'd be getting ready for a tough one and I'd go over to him.

"You owe me one, right?"

"Right."

"Well, I want it tonight."

Then he'd play his heart out.

Today, when I look back in private thoughts, I

enjoy reflecting on some of the things I did which helped win games. And I'm sure Bill, in his private thoughts, enjoys the same type of reflections. Many of those thoughts—his and mine—go hand in hand. We were a lot alike: Two strong personalities, both having the same goals, the same philosophies, both doing anything and everything we could to achieve the triumphs that meant so much to both of us.

I think it's safe to say there's a bond between us that very few men will ever be privileged to share.

I've always wished the public could know the Russell I know, but he's a very private man who's hard to get to know. He just wants to be left alone.

There have been things he's said and done—like refusing to let us formally retire his number, which we did without him; or refusing to attend his own enshrinement in the Hall of Fame—that I have not agreed with, and I've told him so.

Yet throughout his playing days I didn't want to go into his personality or eccentricities unless I felt I had to. That was Russell. That was his thing, so to speak. Other than giving advice where I felt it was welcome or needed, I made no attempt to change him. Who knows? If I had tried to change his personality it might have affected the way he played.

I'll always remember the time I heard him speaking off the cuff to some students at Notre Dame. We were there for an exhibition, as I recall, and it was during the period of great campus upheaval: Civil rights, Vietnam, protests. It seemed students were mad at everyone and raising hell every chance they got.

I watched Bill sit on the edge of a stage and rap with those kids, and all the respect I had for him doubled. He was so articulate, so down-to-earth, so open and honest—and all these kids, including the long hair types, sat with their eyes wide open, fascinated by what they were hearing. I don't know of anybody else in the country who could have held that particular audience under that kind of control. Even today, if he'd go around talking to kids the way he did back then, he'd do a better job of communicating with them than just about anybody else in the nation.

That's the Bill Russell too few people ever get to know.

Will there ever be another Russell?

I don't know. I think the next Dr. J is already here; his name is Michael Jordan. And we might be seeing the next Bob Cousy in Isiah Thomas.

But another Russell? I don't know about that. Patrick Ewing's no Russell. He's a great player and a super kid, but he's a power center; Russell was a finesse center. A guy who'd have a shot at being a Russell-like center if he wasn't so offensive-minded is Ralph Sampson; he's got the quickness, the smarts and the reactions. Akeem Olajuwon? Keep your eyes on him. He might be the one.

I'll always remember what Russell said the first year of his retirement when Kareem Adbul-Jabbar, then known as Lew Alcindor, came into the league with a great flourish. Someone asked Russell, "How would you have done against Alcindor?"

I think that bothered Bill. He was never one to use the word "I" a lot; he never had that kind of ego. But here was this kid, this great offensive machine, creating such a stir that already people were forgetting the way Russell had dominated every center he ever faced.

"The question," he told the interviewer, "is not how I would have done against Alcindor, but rather how Alcindor would have done against me."

It was a great line, and he was absolutely right to have said it.

When you think about it, maybe that's the only way to measure the *next* Bill Russell: How would he have done against the original Bill Russell? Personally, I don't think I'll live to see the man who might have beaten him.

You're always looking, always hoping, to find the next great one, and back in 1977 we started hearing rumors about this kid out at Indiana State. No one ever said he was great at that time, but the word was that he was good, very good. So I watched him on TV a couple of times, and then, during his junior season, I went to see him in person for the first time.

Like Russell, Larry Bird showed me what I wanted to see the first time I laid eyes on him. Here was a kid who could shoot and who knew how to handle the ball. He was going to be eligible for the draft that spring, 1978, even though he was a junior, because he started his collegiate career at Indiana and then sat out a year. But he made it known he intended to play his senior season. Anybody drafting him would have to wait a year. Most teams don't want to do that, but we looked at it differently. Back in 1953 I drafted *three* Kentucky players—Frank Ramsey, Cliff Hagan and Lou Tsioropoulos—a year before they graduated. Like Bird, they were all junior-eligibles.

Why? Because you'd rather have potential *great* fresh blood than potential *good* fresh blood coming into your organization. Any good player you draft probably won't make that big a difference, but a great player can make all the difference in the world. So what's one year? It goes by very quickly, and it's well worth the wait if the player you're talking about has the potential for making a major impact upon your team.

Larry, I felt, had that potential—yet I didn't even dream of the surprises which were to come. I didn't realize how quick he was. I had no knowledge of his rebounding abilities. I knew he had a court presence on offense, but I didn't realize he had one on defense, too. And I had no sense of his leadership qualities, or his ability to motivate other people as well as motivating himself.

I had no great insight into his character, or his personality, or his willingness to play in pain. I have never had an athlete in my 39 years in the league who liked to play more than Larry does and who would make every effort to play, whether he was hurt or not. He symbolizes that old line *if he can walk, he can play* better than any athlete I've ever met.

Yet he was drafted solely on the premise that he

was a damned good ballplayer who could put some points on the board and move the ball around. That's all I was expecting, just as I was only expecting Russell to get us the ball.

We had a terrible season in 1977–78 (32–50) but the one thing it gave us was the sixth pick in the first round. So we waited until the first five names were called: Mychal Thompson, Phil Ford, Rick Robey, Mike Richardson and Purvis Short. Then it was my turn to speak: *Boston takes Larry Bird of Indiana State.*

The following spring, after his senior season, I opened negotiations with his agent, Bob Woolf. They lasted three months and at times were somewhat heated, though a lot of that was just newspaper talk.

I knew Larry was going to cost us some money, and I was prepared to pay a reasonable price, but the point I kept hammering home was that no forward ever *made* a franchise in our league. And historically, I was correct. The only guys who ever had the ability to turn around an entire franchise were centers: Mikan, Russell, Chamberlain, Reed, Jabbar, Walton, Malone. All of your other players, no matter how great they were, were contributors. Look at Dr. J—as great as he is, he didn't win it all until Malone joined him. No forward could do it himself, because forwards are at the mercy of the guards; the guards control the ball.

That's why no forward ever *made* a franchise—until Larry Bird made ours. He was the first exception, and he may go down in history as the only exception.

The day he walked into our rookie camp was the day my eyes were opened: The way he shot the ball; the way he passed it around; the way he crashed the boards; the way he raced up and down the court; the way he controlled the tempo and action; the way he seemed to make *no* mistakes. As I sat there watching, all I could think of was the day Havlicek first showed up 17 years earlier. It was the only thing I could compare it to.

John had just been cut from the Cleveland Browns camp. He flew into town, someone picked him up, and the next thing I knew he was walking onto the court.

Ben Carnevale, the Navy coach, was with me at the time. We started watching John, and after about three minutes I turned to him and said, "Oh my God, what have I got here?" Ben looked at me and said, "I don't know, but I've got a hunch it's going to be something good."

That's how it was with Larry, though maybe not as dramatic—because, remember, I wasn't coaching now. My first thought was simply that this kid was worth every nickel we ended up giving him, which at that time amounted to the richest rookie contract ever signed in any sport.

Larry's very stoic, very unemotional in his expressions, so the more you watch him, the more you appreciate him. He's the consummate pro: He's got a job to do, and anything that might get in the way of doing that job is simply shrugged off, disregarded. Knock him down, he gets back up. He gives as much as he gets in that department. Very seldom does he blow up; diving onto the floor, getting hit with elbows, whatever it is, the look on his face never changes. He just keeps doing the job.

You know what he reminds me of? A street guy with class. That's the only description that keeps coming to my mind: A tough kid off the streets who exudes nothing but class.

I'll tell you something else about him: He's got more mental toughness than any player I've ever seen, including Russell. And I know that Russell has tremendous respect for Bird's ability and for Bird as a person.

There are very few players I would pay to see. I would have paid to see Calvin Murphy play at Niagara. He was spectacular. I'd have paid to see Russell, just to admire the art of his defense. But I wouldn't have paid to see Chamberlain or Jabbar; they don't excite me that way. Don't misunderstand; they're great. But I'd find them monotonous. I wouldn't have paid to see Mikan; he was like a robot. But I'd pay to watch Isiah Thomas, and I'd have paid to watch Dr. J in his prime. Years ago I'd have paid to watch an Elgin Baylor or a Bob Cousy.

As a rule, however, I very rarely jump out of my seat to applaud a player. I guess I've seen too many over the years to react that way anymore. Yet Larry has lifted me out of my seat more than any other player ever has.

It's those moves, that variety of shots, that way he has of improvising as he goes along so that you just don't know what he's going to do, what's coming next. He keeps coming up with the damndest plays I've ever seen. It's like watching Cousy in his prime—yet we're talking about a forward who rebounds like a center!

He is—and I say this unequivocally—the greatest all-around player who ever lived.

Larry's a student of the game in a different way than Russell. Russ might have thought to himself: "If a guy's standing next to me in the pivot here, and I put my hip into him this way, then he can't make the following moves . . ."

Larry doesn't break it down like that. He just sees a shot go up and tells himself: "I'm gonna get it." Yet Bird, in my opinion, would be a better coach than Russell was. Russell hated the nitty-gritty stuff. Even though he loved to think about the game, he hated all the routines.

Bird *sees* what has to be done, *feels* what has to be done, *knows* what has to be done, and he can teach. I've heard him telling things to guys. I've even asked him, on occasion, to explain certain things to players, things I thought they should know which he might not volunteer unless he was asked. He's sensitive to the fact some people might resent it.

Yet he reminds me of something I once heard about Bobby Orr. They say no teammate ever resented a dollar or a drop of ink that came Orr's way, because he was such a team player they all realized how lucky they were to have him on their side. They appreciated his greatness and his humility, and as a result they became his biggest fans.

That's how it is with the Celtics and Bird. They love the guy. Can you blame them?

* * *

From the day Larry started playing in the fall of '79, we haven't had an empty seat in Boston Garden.

People contrast that to the 13 years in which Russell played there, when the average attendance was 8,406.

I don't think the comparison's fair. For years and years we were selling basketball to an area which was predominantly interested in hockey. It took a long time to educate people, to get them to appreciate what our game was all about. And then we started to win with such regularity that our success became a problem, too. What's the point of watching the Celtics? You *know* they're going to win easily. That became a very prevalent mood. It was as if we had become too good for our own good, as ridiculous as that might seem. We were filling houses all around the league, but in Boston no one seemed to get too excited until the playoffs rolled around, and then we played to capacity crowds.

If Bird had played *with* Russell on some of those great teams we had back then, we still wouldn't have sold out. And if Russell had come along five years later, and retired five years later than he did, he'd have been performing for sellout crowds, too. It was just a matter of timing, of educating the public.

I'll say this for Larry, however: He's sold more tickets, as an individual attraction, throughout this league than any player before him. He's become the best box office draw in the history of the NBA. Of all the stars who've made up basketball's galaxy, he shines brightest.

So draft day comes tomorrow and I've got the number one pick of all time. I can have my choice of any player who ever wore an NBA uniform. I can't pick three. I can't pick two. I can pick only one.

So who do I pick: Russell or Bird? They're both *my* guys.

The only way to go about it is coldly and logically. Let's say I take Bird. The next guy takes Russell, and after him it's Walton, Jabbar, Malone and Chamberlain. In that first round, all the top centers go, and then they start in with the greatest forwards and guards.

Meanwhile, I'm left with no center, which means I've got a big problem, assuming I can't win in a league like that with Bird as my center.

See, when I build a ballclub—again, realizing Bird's an exception—my number one priority is my center. My second priority is my guard, the one who's going to be handling the ball most of the time, like a Cousy or an Isiah Thomas. Those are the guys you're going to win or lose with. Then come your forwards.

So, let's say I have Russell as my center: Since everyone else is taking centers, there are still some great forwards around when I get my second pick, though none are quite the same as Bird.

Now let's say I've got Bird as my forward, and I team him with an average center, say a Rich Kelley or a James Edwards.

Would I be better off with the first combination? Or the second? That's what you've got to ask yourself: How am I going to round out my team?

In other words, If I can pair a Russell with a Havlicek, am I going to be better off than I would be with a Bird and some other center?

The answer's got to be yes.

So when they call my name I've got to say: *Boston takes Bill Russell.*

And then I've got to start working on a trade.

4.

Characters on the Sidelines

"It's not what you tell them, but what they hear."

Of all the mistakes a coach can make, I think one of the worst is to fall in love with the sound of his own voice. This is particularly so in basketball. That's why the older I got, the less I talked.

A football coach can go on forever because he's got nine assistants. It's like a board of directors. He does most of his coaching through meetings with members of his staff. Same with baseball. But in basketball and hockey you're dealing primarily with *one* voice, and it's the same voice, day in and day out, for practices, games, pregame talks, intermission talks, team meeting talks, scouting reports, and so on.

Now if this voice has a change of pace, plus some humor, some occasional sarcasm, some force when it's called for, then there's a chance this coach can continue to command his team's attention over a long period of time. But it's not easy.

Let's face it, there are times when you run out of things to say. When that happened to me, I'd cut my pregame talk down to two minutes. Some nights I wouldn't say anything at all. The problem is, when a man becomes a successful coach there's a tendency on his part to want to become a great orator, too. He wants his 15 minutes before the game, *every* game, come hell or high water. When that happens, all of his motivational tactics begin to work against him, because now his players are starting to tune him out. After so many games and so many years, as soon as he stands up to talk they tell themselves: "Here comes his bullshit again." At that point his tirades have lost all of their effectiveness. He's saying things that aren't meaningful just to carry on the conversation.

I'd change the amount of time I talked. Two minutes. Eight minutes. Ten minutes. It varied. And I'd change my inflections as I went along. Sometimes loud. Sometimes soft. Sometimes a combination. Every game was a separate entity.

When it came to communications, my rule of thumb was very simple: *It's not what you tell them, but what they hear.* There's a big difference. If all they hear is a ranter and a raver, a dynamo giving them a staccato bang-bang-bang lecture, they'll listen for a while, but then they're going to shut him off. Invariably, these are the kinds of coaches who end up saying, "I, I, I."

Now it becomes *"my ballclub,"* and *"my team won it,"* or *"you guys lost,"* and *"you guys played lousy."*

The coach begins to believe in his own ego. He starts to think that *he's* winning these games all by himself and that his players are just like pawns in a chess match, which simply isn't so.

You can't be an "I, I, I" coach and be successful very long, not if you're going to be surrounded by the same group of players. They'll just stop producing for you.

I saw what happened to Al Cervi once in Syracuse. He had a good team, but he made the mistake of using the first-person pronoun too often. His players ended up voting him out of a playoff share by a 10–1 count. He got mad and began yelling about it, so Dolph Schayes spoke up. "I just changed my vote," he announced. "Now it's 11–0!" Dolph had originally voted to give him a share out of common courtesy, but Al was a tough guy from the old school who made the mistake of forgetting to realize his players were deserving of some of the credit, too.

Another thing you'll find in some coaches is that they're never at fault. Never. In their minds *they* never lost a game. They never think to themselves: "Maybe I'm not doing a good enough job of teaching. Maybe I'm not substituting well. Maybe there are things that I can improve on." Coaches can lose games, too. But try telling them that.

There's a little-known story behind the story of what might have been the most famous Celtic win of all. I'm talking about Game 7 of our 1965 playoff series against Wilt Chamberlain and the 76ers. We were going for our seventh championship in a row, and with four seconds to go in the final game, Wilt dunked to cut our lead to one, 110–109.

But we had the ball. All we had to do was hold onto it.

Russell, attempting to put it into play, threw it against one of the guide wires supporting the basket.

Philadelphia had done the same thing on an in-bounds play in the opening game of that series. There was a conference after it happened, because no one knew how to call it. I piped up: "The ball has to go to the other team." I won my point and we got the ball. It didn't seem like a big deal at the time, but now my own rule had come back to haunt me. It was Philly's ball, and all of a sudden our championship reign was in peril.

I remember Russ walking into our huddle and saying: "Somebody bail me out. I blew it."

That was typical of him. No excuses. No alibis. But I couldn't let him shoulder all the blame. "Damn it," I told the guys, "it's *my* fault. I made up the damned rule and I should have known better because we're on our own turf."

That, by the way, brings up an important point: You don't bawl them out in the huddle for something that's already transpired. You can't waste your time doing that. You have to use that time to discuss what's going to happen next, which is what we did.

We didn't *plan* for John Havlicek to steal the ball on the inbounds pass, of course. We simply went over assignments and reminded ourselves to stay cool.

But if we hadn't pulled it out, no matter what Russ said, I was prepared to accept the blame, and that's what I would have told the press.

I can remember walking into our locker room on many occasions and telling my guys: "Hey, you didn't play that badly, but I stunk tonight. I don't know why, but I just wasn't up, I was half asleep out there . . ."

I could see their eyes light up. They appreciated that.

Then there'd be other nights when a Russell, a Ramsey, or someone like that would come over after a win and say, "Damn, you were masterful on that bench tonight!" When that happened I'd be 10 feet high, because I knew they meant it. They were sincere people.

I never wanted to show anybody how smart I was. Contrary to my public image, I was laid back in many ways.

I never read a basketball book. Oh, I've flipped through a lot of them, but whenever I come to the X's and O's I skip right past them. See, most mistakes that occur in a basketball game are just commonsense mistakes, sometimes made out of obvious stupidity. It's not a complicated game. I made up my mind a long time ago that much of this written stuff—the X's and O's— has no real purpose whatsoever other than to make the author look smart.

I see this all the time at coaching clinics. When you give a talk or a speech, it's very important to communicate with your listeners on their level, in language they can understand. You're not up there to impress them. You're there to share ideas with them. The idea is not for them to sit there and marvel over how brilliant you are; the idea is for them to absorb what you have to say. Yet so many coaches get up in clinics and try to put everything on a very high level, making it sound extremely complicated. Why? Because they're hoping to gain the respect of their audience by demonstrating how much they know.

That was never my theory. My idea was to make sure the audience walked away with at least one thing it would remember, even if it was something as simple as remembering to lift up your head when you shoot the ball. I figured if they took one thing back to their programs with them, then they'd have had a profitable time.

It goes back to what I said before: *It's not what you tell them, but what they hear.*

I just tried to talk about the game of basketball. I never tried to sell myself.

One of the things that upsets me most today is the way some of these coaches are starting to call out every play, just like they do in football. That's one of the reasons why I've always felt football lacks imagination. You talk about robots! When Paul Brown coached Cleveland he sent in every play. His guys weren't even allowed to think for themselves.

I understand football's different. Maybe it's the nature of the game. You send some guy with binoculars up to the press box, then he gets on the phone to the coach down on the field and tells him: "Someone's missing an assignment, so let's run this play." I can see that happening once in a while. You've got enough time to talk things over.

But I still feel there's something missing when a quarterback doesn't call most of the plays. If he's bright—and to be a quarterback you can't be stupid—he'll have a feel for what's happening on the field, a feel that the guy in the press box couldn't possibly have. He'll see things from up there, but there's no way he can have a *feel* for them. I like a situation where a guy on the line comes running into the huddle and says: "Run that goddamn ball past me. I'll kill that SOB this time!" But see, he doesn't have a chance to say that, because the next play's coming in from the sidelines. I want the guy in the huddle to be saying to the quarterback: "Look, I can beat this guy and I know it. I'll fake him once and

. . ." That may happen, but while the quarterback's making his decision, boom, here comes another play from the guy with the binoculars. To me, that's a big problem in football.

And now it's getting to be a problem in basketball, too. Watch some of these coaches; they're on their feet all night, shouting instructions, and what they're really doing is killing the creativity of their players, taking away the free-spiritedness which makes basketball such a fun game to play and such a fun game to watch. They're beginning to run it like a football game and it really annoys me.

They're pacing back and forth, yelling: "Okay, if you've got the break, take it. But if you're not sure, don't take it; look at me." Hell, tell a team that and it feels handcuffed.

I watch guys like Hubie Brown, Don Nelson, Jack Ramsay—good coaches, no question about that—and they seem to be calling out most of the plays, as if the players were stupid or something.

Why can't the players call the play? The only time I can see a coach giving his team a play is during a timeout, unless it's a very unusual situation. Otherwise, all you're doing is interrupting the fluidity of the game. The other team misses a shot, you get the rebound, and the first thing you've got to do is look at your coach. He's going to give you a signal. And now you run that play. Meanwhile, one of your teammates might have been free at the other end of the floor. So some of these coaches modify their strategy: "If a guy's free, throw it to him. If not, hold it up, look at me and I'll tell you what to run." That's not the game of basketball as I know it.

I'll tell you what it is. It's basketball where the coach has begun to upstage the players. The coach knows he's on TV, he knows the cameras are going to be panning the sidelines, so he's all over the place, doing these crazy things.

Like these guys with their clipboards. That drives me bananas.

We used to practice game conditions. We'd divide

the squad into two groups, then tell the Greens: "Okay, you're two points down, the Whites have the ball, and there are 10 seconds to go. You—you're the captain; what do you tell them?" I'd listen as they discussed it. Then we'd all talk about it. Situation after situation, we'd do the same thing until we knew the plays we wanted to use and their execution became second nature.

We didn't panic and start bringing out clipboards to draw up emergency plays. How the hell are you going to do that in 30 seconds, with the crowds yelling and everyone feeling tense? That's no time for a new play. That's the time you go to something you're familiar with. That's why we practiced and practiced specific situations so that we wouldn't have to panic when it came down to the closing seconds. I expected each man on the floor to know how much time was left, how many fouls he'd committed, how many fouls the man he was guarding had committed. Then we'd just select a play, and I'd tell them quietly, "Okay, you know what you've got to do."

That's so much better than ranting and raving, adding to the overall confusion. What you want to do at a time like that is remain calm, collect your thoughts, and concentrate on executing your strategy properly.

When I see a coach waving his clipboard, furiously drawing diagrams, I see a coach who's selling himself to the TV cameras, selling himself to the crowd, when what he should be doing is selling his team. And you see an extension of that in the locker room where these same coaches are monopolizing the postgame interviews, getting themselves quoted for the next day's papers.

I used to spend five minutes in our locker room, that's all. Then I'd leave. I'd tell the writers: "Hey, those guys played the game. Ask them." But that's not the way it works today. Not as a rule, though KC Jones is one of the best at not upstaging his players. It's just one more thing I love about the guy.

Basketball, as I've pointed out, is a free-spirited game, a game of touch and feel. I hate to see a player, after he's made a mistake. immediately look over to his coach, as if waiting for a reaction.

And I hate to see a coach pull a player out of a game immediately after a mistake. First, it's embarrassing to the player. Second, you're going to end up with a nervous player. Some coaches don't care if they embarrass a player, and some don't realize that their heavy-handedness is very counterproductive. They think what they're doing is making the player more aware of his mistakes, which is true enough. But at the same time they're making him nervous, and you don't want nervous ballplayers. You want happy ballplayers. You can be happy and still play with great intensity. Nervous ballplayers lose their touch, lose their natural desire to make things happen out there on the court. They begin playing scared, and that's not the way this game is supposed to be played.

A coach can make a player scared. A coach can inhibit a player. A coach can *ruin* a player. And for what? To show everybody who's boss? Some coaches feel, "I don't care if my players hate me, as long as they do what I tell them to do."

But when I was coaching, I didn't want anybody to hate me. Certainly not my own players! All I wanted was their respect, and you don't get respect through yelling at people and embarrassing them.

That's what's known as coaching through fear. It's not only a lousy way to coach, it also doesn't work in the long run.

There's another type of fear in coaching. That's when the coach is afraid of the stars.

Let's say a guy has great success as a high school coach and now he's about to move up a notch and coach at the college level. Before he does anything else, he's got to make up his mind to get one point across in a hurry: "Hey, most of you guys are my age—but it's *my* job, and if I'm going to lose it because we're not successful, it'll be because my ideas didn't work, not because you disagreed with those ideas. And it doesn't matter if you're a better player than I was back in college. That doesn't matter at all. What matters is that

I've prepared myself to do a good job here. You're a
player. I'm the coach. So you're either going to do
things my way or you're not going to play. That way, if
we're unsuccessful, it'll be my own fault I'm not
successful."

I'm not saying a good coach doesn't listen to his
players' ideas and respect their feel for what's taking
place in a game. If he has any brains at all, he'll want to
know what they think and encourage their suggestions.
What I'm talking about here is discipline. You have to
have discipline to make a program go. And what is
discipline? Discipline is just a proper response to authority. That's all. You can have great discipline without imposing a thousand rules. It's like I always told my
guys: "I live in a democracy and I believe in democracy, but you can't have democracy in sports because
there isn't time for one. So my word is law."

But I liked to think of myself as a benevolent
dictator.

Take my good friend Matt Zunic. We played together one year at George Washington; I was a senior
and he was a sophomore. He went on to become an
honorable mention All-American and had a much better college career than I did. He later joined the Washington Caps and I was his coach. They called him Mad
Matt in college, which gives you some idea of his fiery
nature.

The first time I pulled him out of a game he came
storming over to me and asked: "What the hell did you
do that for?"

I told him to sit down. Then after a couple of
minutes I called him over and pointed to the seat next
to me on the bench. He sat down again.

"I want to tell you something," I said. "I'm coaching, so it's my job on the line. I hired you, and I can
fire you so goddamn fast your head will spin. Don't you
ever let me see a demonstration like that again when I
tell you to come out of a game. I don't have to give you
a reason. Maybe I want to rest you. Maybe I think
someone else could do a better job in a certain situation. Maybe a million things. I don't want you throwing

your jacket, or throwing a towel, or saying one damn word to me. Understand? There's just one thing I want you to do when I take you out of a ballgame, and that's to sit down and shut up."

He heard me. So did all of the other players, which was just as important. We never had a problem again.

Later, when I was coaching the Celtics, we brought Arnie Risen—a veteran at Rochester for many years—onto the team as a backup center. The following season he did a tremendous job of helping Russell, then a rookie, learn the ways of the NBA.

Well, I had rules for our huddles. One rule was that I didn't want anybody sitting down. I wanted to show contempt for the other team. *They* had to sit down. *They* were tired. *They* needed rest. But *we* were in superb physical condition. The Boston Celtics were not tired! It was just a little bit of psychology, but, hey, every little bit helps. I wanted them to know we were ready to run right back out there and chase their asses up and down the court. It was like Muhammad Ali standing in his corner between rounds, just staring in disgust at his opponent who was so weak he had to sit on a stool.

Another rule I had was that I didn't want anybody talking unless he was asked to talk. A timeout lasted a minute. There was no time for group conversation.

Well, Arnie was one of the sweetest guys you'd ever want to meet, but in Rochester the team more or less ran itself during huddles. So he walked into our huddle one night and started yapping about something. Everyone else looked at me with horror in their eyes: "How can *he* talk now? *No one* talks now!"

I didn't want to bawl him out. You've got to know the personalities you're dealing with. So I spoke very softly. "Arnie," I said, interrupting him, "I want to tell you something. You guys did many strange things in Rochester. But over here we have an axiom, a very simple rule that's not hard to understand: You play. I coach. In other words, in common everyday language, *keep your goddamn mouth shut!*"

He never did it again.

We had a similar situation when Willie Naulls joined us in 1963. We were playing lousy that night and I was mad, so as soon as we went into our huddle I jumped on Willie: "Damn it, Willie, I told you to box under those boards!"

At that point he interrupted me: "I tried to, but I got caught in a switch . . ."

That's when I let him have it. "I don't want to hear any goddamn speeches from you. I told you to do something. If you can't do it, then sit down! I don't want to hear 'why' from you. I don't care why. And I don't want any talking in this huddle unless you're asked to talk."

It was a strong put-down, even by my standards of handling those matters, and I felt kind of bad as soon as I said it. Willie hadn't meant any disrespect by what he said, but it was a point I had to make very clear.

Later that night I called him aside in our locker room. "Let me explain what happened out there," I said, "just so there won't be any more problems. When I tell you something in a huddle, or if I'm bawling you out in a huddle, I don't have time to go into any long dissertations. The whole timeout lasts only a minute. I told you that you weren't boxing out, and you tried to tell me that you got caught in a switch. First of all, we both know you never boxed out very well anyway, so in all probability I was right. But even if I wasn't right, I don't want any discussions like they have on other teams. There's no time for them. That's why I gave you hell out there."

He said he understood, and I never had another problem with him, either.

From the very first day I coached at St. Alban's Prep in Washington, I realized the number one thing I had to do was get my players to believe in me, to trust my judgment, to have confidence in the fact that I knew what I was talking about.

Let's take players' weight, for example. I don't know how many times I've seen a college team with great personnel get beaten by lesser teams simply because its players were not properly conditioned. What's the matter with these coaches? Why don't they smarten up?

You'd think, for instance, if they saw a Tommy Heinsohn playing at 234 in college, then watched him play so much better in the pros at 216, it might open their eyes. Frank Ramsey was an All-American at Kentucky at 205, then became a Hall of Famer with us at 190. I can think of all kinds of examples.

Take Adrian Dantley. He's sort of a protégé of mine, coming from Washington. One day I took him aside and told him: "Adrian, you're strong enough to play this game whether you're 250 or 200, so take some weight off." He was about 235 at the time. I suggested he get down to about 218, which he did. This is a great kid. He'd have been a Celtic, but there was never any way I could get him. So he came back to me one day and said, "I did it." "Great," I told him. "How do you feel? Better?" He said he did. He started playing better, and I never said another word to him. Then one day he came over to me again. "You know," he said, "I think I'm going to take off *more* weight." And I said: "Fine. As long as you're comfortable and you feel it'll make you quicker, go ahead."

He got down as low as 205 that year and won the league scoring championship.

Now why don't other coaches see this? Why don't they see how a Rick Robey, who weighed 255 in college, did his best playing in the pros when he weighed 240?

Why don't they go to a kid who weighs 250 and tell him: "Look, you need your quickness. You don't need this baby fat. Let me run it off for you. Watch your diet. Let's play at 235."

I'll tell you why they don't do it. When a kid's a real good player in college, a star, there's an element of fear in the minds of many coaches, fear that if they get on his case he might quit; he might say: "Who needs this? I'm a hell of a player! So I'll sit out a year and transfer." So the coaches back off. And they make a big mistake when they do that.

Of course, the great ones won't back off. The Dean Smiths, the John Thompsons, the Bobby Knights—they all do what has to be done. They're great believers in discipline. They understand, as all good coaches do, that no player is bigger than the team. Remember when John suspended Michael Graham from his national championship team? It wasn't because he didn't care for the kid. John cares for all of his kids. It was simply a matter of doing what had to be done in light of his rules and regulations.

Now *that's* great coaching!

No player is bigger than the team. Once a player becomes bigger than the team, you no longer have a team.

Maybe it's an ego thing, but some coaches seem reluctant to copy other coaches' ideas. That's crazy. I never tried to tell my guys that I knew it all, that I had all the answers. I'd tell them, "I know *enough*, but I don't know it all, so if somebody else comes up with a good idea, hell, let's steal it!"

Oh, I tried to be innovative, too. A lot of the out-of-bounds plays you see in the league today were mine to begin with. Some of them came from players' suggestions. Others were invented out on the playgrounds of Washington. On Saturdays and Sundays in the off-season there'd be lots of college and NBA players hooking up in scrimmages. I'd say; "Hey guys, I've got an idea. Let's try this out." If it worked on a playground, why couldn't it work in the NBA? So I'd set them up in a certain way, then ask myself: "Would the referees call three-seconds if we lined up like this?" We'd test it. "No," I'd say, "because the clock doesn't start until someone touches the ball, and by that time the shot will be gone, so they *can't* call three-seconds."

A lot of plays were developed that way, by thinking ahead and experimenting. But, again, if I saw something good? Copy it!

The trouble with most coaches today is that they don't study a situation before reacting to it. That means studying the referees, too. Know them. Know what they like and don't like. Know what they'll call and what they'll allow. Then figure out how far you can go.

You've got to pick your spots. That's what it all comes down to. But some of these guys—they're up on *every* call. Now, come on, the ref can't be wrong *every* time, can he? So after a while who can blame him for thinking: "Hey, this guy's been busting my chops all night. I'll fix him. The hell with that."

Sure, early in my career, when I was going through the learning process, I picked up a lot of technicals. I made mistakes. Then sometimes I'd purposely get a T, just to show the players that I was behind them.

I still have an image as a guy who was on his feet all night, storming the court, bitching over calls, raising hell wherever he could. But that just wasn't so. The longer I coached, the more I learned to pick my spots, sometimes arguing only in order to put a bug in the ref's mind for the *next* call.

Today, many of your coaches—football, basketball, hockey, all of them—want to bitch about everything, and pretty soon they end up with a reputation among the officials which only hurts their ballclubs.

When Tommy Heinsohn was coaching for us, he learned to pick his spots—but sometimes, when things got hot, he'd overdo it a bit. I'd tell him: "Tommy, make sure you're right. Pick your spots! Don't object to a call when you know in your heart you're wrong. You can't be climbing all over a guy when you don't really believe what you're saying."

That's one of the secrets I try to tell young coaches today: Be *sure* you're right if you plan to strenuously object. Hey, take it from an old coach. Some of these guys are a pain in the ass, and I don't blame the officials for tossing them out on their ears!

Watch Bobby Knight. I know, he's got a reputation for being a hothead. So did I. But Bobby knows how to pick his spots. He'll go through many games without saying a word. Of course, no one ever writes about that. But if he feels the referee is being influenced by the other coach, then sure—he'll be on his feet in a minute, doing his damndest to *un*-influence him. If he gets a T in a situation like that, then it's what I'd call a calculated T, designed to tell the officials: "Hey, I'm here, too! You're not going to crap on me."

That's not making a nuisance of yourself. That's just smart coaching.

To me, Bobby Knight is a brilliant tactician, a brilliant motivator. He takes every single little percentage he can get. For a number of years he'd ask me, or his buddy Havlicek, to make a three-minute motivational cassette which he'd play for his team in special situations. When he was coaching the Olympic team he called me up and asked me to say a few words at one of their practices. I didn't have anything much to say. Whatever I did say, I'm not sure it mattered at all. But if he felt it gave him one-tenth of a one percent edge, that was enough to make him happy.

He's a thinker. I was a thinker. That's one of the reasons I like him so much.

The press doesn't like him, but that's because he's not a newspaper coach. He doesn't spend a lot of time trying to sell himself; his kids are the only thing he cares about. So he gets knocked a lot. After one of his Olympic wins, a writer at the press conference said something to Bobby about his squad's great teamwork. I loved his answer: "Yeh, I'd like to see ten of you egomaniacs get together to write a column!"

Diplomatic? No. But I thought it was funny as hell.

The press doesn't like John Thompson either, but I have a tremendous regard for him—not just because he played for the Celtics, but because I know he's a man of high principle and great moral character.

John went to Georgetown and did what he had to do: He went out and got some players. And he cares deeply for every one of those kids, even those he's suspended. He looks out for them. Hey, maybe he *is* overprotective, as some of his critics claim. He's made some mistakes along that route. But at the same time, he realizes that a lot of these kids are going to be misquoted, and he knows what that can do to the morale of a team. Some of them are young and immature, and reporters have a way of unsettling people they talk with. So even though the media climbs all over his back, John has been big enough and strong enough and tough enough to stand up to all of them, at the expense of his own P.R., and deny them the total access they demanded.

I admire him for that, I really do. He could have made himself a hero by opening the doors to his locker room and posing for all of the cameras, submitting to all of the interviews. That would have been the easy way out. He could have become a media darling. Instead, he has stood firmly on a principle, even at his own expense. That's *great* coaching.

Yet he's man enough to back off when he's wrong. I said to him one day: "John, do you realize what you guys are doing?"

"What do you mean?" he asked.

Without realizing it, he'd taken his team off the court for last-minute instructions just before "The Star-Spangled Banner." This was at a time when a lot of kids were sitting through the anthem, raising their fists. It was disgusting, but it was becoming a trend.

"John," I told him. "Not at this time! You can't do that at this particular time. People might get the idea you're a militant."

He thought about that for a minute, then agreed.

Actually, we've got the same situation in Boston with Cedric Maxwell. Max is no militant, but he went to the john before the anthem several years ago, and then it became a superstition. If I thought he was making a statement I'd have landed on him long ago. But he isn't. So I let it go, even though it bothers me a bit. I know enough about ballplayers to understand that you don't screw around with their superstitions unless you have to.

I'll tell you another coach I like. Dean Smith. He's also got a reputation for being a very honorable guy. He wants no part of any shenanigans. And like Bobby and John, he's vitally concerned with the well-being of his kids.

Dean's known for very free substitutions. When a kid goes down there to play for him, he's going to get his playing time, no matter who he is. Dean can be feisty, but he's a good, smart coach who stands up for what he believes in, who's not afraid to take a position when he knows he's right. That's so important in my book.

There are a lot of great coaches out there—Denny Crum; Lou Carnesecca; Eddie Sutton; Joe B. Hall; Lefty Driesell; that kid up in Syracuse, Jim Boeheim— but if I had to pick the three best in the country, those are the three I'd pick: Bobby, John and Dean.

Ask *any* of those guys I just mentioned to tell you where any of his kids are today. He'll know. That's the kind of loyalty and caring that makes someone a great coach. All of the great ones know.

Of course, when you talk about the great college coaches you have to include John Wooden. John's a good friend of mine, and I respect him as perhaps the greatest college coach who ever lived. I mean that.

But I've always had an axe to grind with UCLA: *Why didn't any of those great ballplayers represent this country in Olympic basketball?*

Stop and think about it. Why? Was it because John wasn't named the Olympic coach? Was it because they didn't care? Was it because he didn't have that kind of control over them? Why? Where was Jabbar, or Alcindor as he was known then? Where was Walton? Where were the great UCLA stars when their country was putting its reputation on the line? Where the hell were those guys?

I don't hold John accountable for that, but I *do* hold the school accountable. I think UCLA's record in this regard is disgraceful.

And please don't give me any of that crap about the school being located in a very radical political atmosphere. Bull. The school's located in America, and that should be enough.

Kentucky kids played. Indiana kids played. Dean Smith's kids played. From Michigan, Ohio, all over the place, the great players played and made their country proud. All except the kids from UCLA. Where the hell were they?

They stayed home. Because they were spoiled. And because they lacked the patriotism that, in my opinion, they should have had. That's always disturbed me. It still does. And, though I'll be the first to admit they've played some magnificent basketball there, I'll never forgive them for ducking what should have been their greatest honor of all.

5.

An Owner's Manual

"The straw that nearly broke this camel's back."

One of my favorite expressions has always been: *A little knowledge is a dangerous thing.* And over the years, no one's proved that more to me than the owners who've come into our game.

Don't misunderstand, some of them have been outstanding. But there have been too many terrible ones, guys who've been in it strictly for the recognition, to soothe their own egos. Once they've done that, boom, they revert back to habit: "I can sell the club now for a pretty good profit, so let's get the hell out of here!"

Who are they? Where do they come from?

Well, let's say a man makes millions of dollars in some business, some private industry. Say he's worth $50 million. What is it he can do for $60 million that he can't do for $50 million? He's got enough money to do any damned thing he pleases. So he takes some of that money and decides he's going to have a hobby. Since he likes sports a little bit, he tells himself, "I think I'll buy a franchise. I may lose a million or two a year, but so what? I'm making more than that in interest on my other money, and it's a write-off anyway."

So he buys a franchise, and he tells himself, "I'm a pretty smart guy. I did pretty well with my business, didn't I? So why can't I be just as smart here?" The result? He becomes a meddler.

I've always believed that any time there's a sizable amount of money involved in a decision you've got to go to the owner to make sure he's in agreement. That's only reasonable; it's his money, he has a right to know what's being done with it. It doesn't mean, however, that he should start making the basketball decisions.

I'll give you a good example. One of the many owners we've had in Boston was a man named Marvin Kratter, who was chairman of the board at National Equities, a big company in New York with a lot of holdings, primarily in real estate. I liked Marvin. I still do. In fact, I've gone into some investments with him since he sold the club in 1968.

He was a business-building genius, a super salesman, a brilliant man who also had a large ego. He'd bring clients up to Boston to see a game and use his company jet. But instead of having someone in our office phone ahead to the restaurant where they'd be eating, Marvin loved to call from the plane, halfway between Boston and New York, and order right there from the menu. Things like that. And, of course he'd have limousines waiting for his entourage when they arrived at the airport.

That's the way he was, and I kind of got a kick out of him. It wasn't *me*. No way. That's never been my style. But it was fun to watch and he was fun to be around—except when I felt his outgoing manner was detrimental to our operation.

I remember one time when Bailey Howell got something in his eye, a very minor situation. I said we'd have our own ophthalmologist look at it, but, no, Marvin starts yelling, "Hey, we've got a great eye doctor down in New York; let's get him down there!" He scared poor Baily half to death.

One time he had a direct phone line installed from his office in New York to my office in Boston, just so we could "keep in touch." Well, I knew what that meant.

Marvin was a fan, and he'd be on that phone five or six times a day if I didn't do something about it. So every time he called I made believe the phone was out of order on my end. Finally I said, "Marvin, this damn thing's never working. Let's get it out of here." It was gone after a couple of weeks.

Yet he was very good to me personally. He took out a big policy on my life and told me he never would have bought the club if I hadn't been a part of the deal. Hey, that would make anyone feel good. Still, I was the type of manager he couldn't very well mold, not the way he could other divisional heads of his corporation. In sports you have to fly by the seat of your pants.

One day, just before an expansion draft, he calls a meeting of all his department heads at his office in the Pan-Am Building in New York. There they are, his board of directors, and there I am, sitting with them. Pretty soon I discover that the purpose of this meeting is to decide which players we're going to protect in the upcoming draft. I can't believe it! I start to say something, but Marvin waves me off: "Not yet, Red. In a minute."

He turns to one of his vice-presidents. "What do you think of not protecting Nelson and Sanders?"

The guy says, "Well, Marvin, you know what you're doing. If you think that's okay, I go along with you."

He turns to the next guy, who tells him, "I'm not totally in accord on not protecting Sanders, but I'll go along with Nelson." Meanwhile, I'm going nuts.

Finally he calls on Jack Waldron, the only one who showed me any guts. "Marvin," he says, "the only thing I can say is that you're paying Red a lot of money to run the team. Don't you think we ought to hear what he has to say?"

Now, at last, it's my turn. I get up and I'm hot. Really steamed.

"You mean I can actually have the floor?"

They all look at me like they know what's coming.

"I don't know what the hell is going on here," I tell them. "But this is the damndest thing I've ever seen in my life. You guys discussing the skills of basketball players is like having a group of civilians run a war. It's ridiculous. A joke. You're talking to your friends, talking to people you know, and coming back with all their crazy opinions. Having you guys run a draft would be like asking me to pick out a piece of real estate and tell you what it's worth. I wouldn't do that. I wouldn't presume to do it. I wouldn't have the balls to sit here and tell you people how to run your business. But that's exactly what you've been doing to me—and if this is how you plan to run things, then you can take your ballclub and shove it! I want no part of it. And I'll issue a release to the press immediately, saying I've got nothing to do with what's about to happen."

"Red, Red," Marvin says. "Don't get so excited." He puts his arm around me and takes me over to the window. "Look," he says. "Isn't that a beautiful view?"

I told him what he could do with his view.

"I'm not here to look at any damn views," I said. "I'm here to get something squared away. And, Marvin, I meant what I said." Then I left.

They eventually came around to my way of thinking, but that's what I mean by a little knowledge being a dangerous thing.

In addition to meddling, the other thing that happens when a man buys a franchise is that now he begins to get his picture into the newspapers. All of a sudden reporters are calling him up for stories. He's being quoted all over town, and before you know it his head starts becoming a little bigger. I don't have to give any examples of that: Just look around, there are plenty to choose from. And this just adds fuel to the notion: "Hey, so what if I haven't been around very long? I'm as smart as any of these GMs. Look at the money I've made. Doesn't that prove it? What the hell have *they* ever made? They work for me!"

When a man starts thinking that way, his franchise is in trouble.

Once in a while you run into an owner who really does know something about the game. But too many of them are influenced by their families and their friends, and as a result, like fans, they begin to form likes and dislikes. They become overly concerned with stats; some of them read them voraciously. Stats: That's the ultimate! Stats have always been a pet peeve of mine. Always.

They're not concerned with what a man does in the clutch. They're not concerned with things he does on the court that can't be measured in statistics, like defensive ability. They may be interested in steals, but they fail to realize that for every steal you make you may also be giving up a big basket by taking that gamble. But, see, they're not interested in any of this because it can't be measured in stats. They also don't see a guy play on the road, where it's a lot harder to come up with the consistent big effort.

So all of this stuff is going through their minds, along with all of the crap they're hearing from their pals at the country club, and now they want to argue with their GM and their coach when it comes to determining the worth of a player, having no idea at all of what that player's real worth is or what he means to the chemistry of the team.

Unfortunately, much of your destiny rides on the ownership of your team. As a rule, I was strong enough, without being too adamant, to get what I wanted, especially when it came to the good of the Celtics. We've had a lot of owners over the years; some good, some not so good at all. And we've made a lot of money for all of them. As each one came along I'd tried to understand his philosophy, his motives, his objectives: *Why did he buy the team?* And I'd try my best to fit in with his line of thinking, up to a point, but not to where it would destroy the ballclub. I'd try to go along with him on the things which weren't important and things which were important to him but not to me. And if he wanted input, fine; I listened. But that didn't mean I was going to agree.

What I tried to do was make them feel important. I'd tell them, "Look, I won't make any deals unless you're aware of them, and when I do, I'll give you the reasons why." That never bothered me. I never had the kind of ego which said: "I'm the *only* one in charge here." No way. When a man has hundreds of thousands of his own dollars on the line, he has every right to know what is going on and why.

What you've got to have—what you *hope* to have—is a situation in which everyone's pulling together in the same direction, toward the same goals. That means not only having an owner who's a fan, but one who cares about his people and his organization, who's not in it solely for the recognition or to make a quick profit. Ideally, you want someone who loves the game and enjoys his association with it, even while recognizing his own limitations. My definition of a good owner is someone who'll do what successful executives in other fields do: Hire the best people, then stick by them.

What happens too often is that they begin to feel the personnel man is a nonessential guy, so they start talking directly to the coaches, bypassing their own GM. They think they're smart enough to do the job themselves and invariably they wind up making big mistakes.

Things have been getting a little bit better lately, but for a while there I was becoming so aggravated by what I saw and heard at league meetings that I threatened not to attend them anymore.

The people who attended those meetings never talked about the game. They didn't give a damn about the game. All they wanted to know was, "How much are we going to be getting from TV?" Or, "What about such-and-such litigation?" Or, "What about that guy who's suing us?"

That's all you ever heard. No one talked about the referee situation. No one talked about proposed rule changes. That kind of stuff was swept under the rug. It was just a business to these people, and the only thing that really excited them was seeing their pictures in the paper.

The oldtimers, the pioneers, the owners who put this league onto its feet—Walter Brown, Eddie Gottlieb, Ned Irish—never worried about perpetuating their own images or taking bows for their great contributions to the sport. They were above that kind of crap. They were sportsmen in the true sense of the word, and the people who've come onto the scene in later years just haven't been as classy.

Some won't spend a dime. I've always said it's not how much a guy has, but how much he's willing to spend. They're all millionaires. One might be worth $100 million. The other's worth only $8 million or $9 million—but he'll spend it, while the guy with $100 million won't.

Then there are others who spend like fools. These guys burn me most of all because what they've done is capitulate to the players to the detriment of the game. They think if only they get so-and-so onto their team it will get them over the hump; they'll win it all. They don't realize that it doesn't work that way. Meanwhile they're going crazy.

It all started with David Thompson, when Denver, worried about losing him, gave him around $400,000 *more* than they had to, something like an $800,000 package, which was practically unheard of back then. What happens? They never win a thing with David Thompson. Meanwhile they've destroyed everyone else's economics.

That's why I've always admired NFL owners. Basically, they have unity. Much more than our owners do. Our guys are primarily selfish. But if they want to blow their dough, I suppose it's their right to do so.

I've seen situations where two teams will make a deal—tit for tat, swapping two players who are equal in ability—and then all of a sudden one owner will realize he's about to spend another $300,000 a year in salary that he hadn't figured on. For three years! That's an extra $1 million going out of his pocket, and he hasn't improved his team a bit. That doesn't bother some of these people at all. Me? It would drive me crazy.

I had a situation in 1972 where a deal I made— giving our NBA rights to Charlie Scott to Phoenix in exchange for Paul Silas—was almost negated behind my back. At the time we had just begun operating under another new ownership—the previous one had disappeared in a Chapter 11 bankruptcy claim—and I guess the people in Phoenix, after getting all kinds of heat from their fans, realized they'd made a mistake in letting Silas go. At first they offered us $150,000 to buy him back. We said no, no way, nothing doing. Then, unbeknownst to me, Dick Bloch, their owner, calls our new owner and ups the offer to $250,000—and our guy wants to take it! He calls me to tell me what's about to happen, and I say, "Whoa, you can't play dollar bills." Then I tried to make him understand what Silas would mean to our team—we won two championships with him!—and I also pointed out that without Silas the team wouldn't be worth as much if these new guys decided that they wanted to sell the franchise.

He backed off and said, "Fair enough, you're running the team. I just didn't know that much about it." That was Steve Haymes, a reasonable guy.

But see how the game is played? Rather than going through me, which they knew would be a waste of time, the Phoenix people go right to our new owners, figuring they're businessmen who don't know what's going on when it comes to basketball. And they almost got away with it.

I can remember so many times when I'd be sitting at a league meeting, listening to these people go on and on about things which had nothing to do with the game itself, thinking, "What about basketball? Isn't that what we're supposed to be here for?" Meanwhile, they've all rented fancy suites and set up hospitality rooms and it's party time. It used to drive me nuts. It still does sometimes.

What they should do is sit down for a couple of days and listen to the suggestions and recommendations of the Competition & Rules Committee. This is what it's all about. A good recommendation will come out and you'll have owners saying, "Nah, we don't like that one." And they'll knock it down. What in hell do they know about the damned game that qualifies them to knock down a rule? But they've got to have that input, see? That's their egos at work again. Or sometimes they'll turn thumbs down on a good suggestion because of personal prejudices: "If so-and-so wants a rule, it must be good for *his* team, so I'd better vote against it." They assume everyone's got an ulterior motive and that's not always so. Sure, I want what's good for the Celtics, but I care about the league as well. So did Walter Brown when he owned the team. There were many times when Walter voted in favor of something that he believed was for the good of the league, even after I tried to convince him it would victimize his own ballclub. That's the kind of guy he was.

Some rules just make sense, no matter who proposes them. I know. I've put a lot of them through, like elimination of the jump ball at the start of every quarter. I maintained it was unfair. If you're playing some team who's got a guy 7–2, 7–4 or whatever, he's going to control the tap all four times. That means you may be spotting the other side, say, six points, figuring four possessions should be worth that much to a good team. That's a pretty big spot, especially if it happens to be a decent team you're playing. I contend you should start the game even, and there are too many factors involved in a jump ball. For one thing, most referees do a lousy job of tossing up the ball. They're afraid of getting hit, so most of them are backing off as they toss it up. And then you get guys who are cute, like Tom Boerwinkle was. He got almost every tap because he used to cheat! He'd hit guys on the way up. Here's a guy who couldn't jump three inches, controlling every tap because he knew a couple of tricks.

My idea was that we should do what football does. One team gets the ball to start the first half, then the other team gets it to start the second half. That's only fair. Otherwise, all a team would have to do is find some giant about 7–6 to grab the tap, then call time out and get him out of there. He'd be contributing six points a night even though he couldn't play. It'd be a joke.

Rules, Referees. This is what the game is all about. If more owners understood that, we'd all be better off.

*   *   *

Then there was John Y. Brown, the straw that nearly broke this camel's back.

John and his partner, Harry Mangurian, owned the Buffalo Braves at the same time Irv Levin and his partner, Harold Lipton, owned the Celtics. John wanted out of Buffalo. He looked at several cities and finally decided on San Diego. Irv, meanwhile, was a California guy who wanted to stay in the NBA, but not necessarily in Boston, particularly after the fans in the Garden gave him a good going over on John Havlicek's retirement day. That was in April 1978. Our record that year was 37–50, and no one in Boston was happy. I couldn't blame them.

Brown and Levin got together and made a deal to swap franchises. Levin went to San Diego with the Braves, who were renamed the Clippers, and Brown came to Boston. The transaction included not just the ballclubs, but some individual members of the teams, too. Kermit Washington, Kevin Kunnert and our second first-round pick that year, Freeman Williams—the first was Larry Bird; thank God they didn't take him—went to San Diego, and Tiny Archibald, Marvin Barnes and Billy Knight came to us. That was the first time in all my years in Boston that a player transaction had been made without my knowledge.

I learned about all of this in a phone call I got from Brown, and by the time I hung up I realized this ownership was going to be different from anything I'd ever experienced before.

John was flamboyant, to say the least, and we clashed right from the start. I never questioned his right to do the crazy things he did; he was the owner, and I always acknowledged that. But I'd tell him, "John, you and I have different personalities, different theories, and if you don't sell the team I'm going to leave." I also told him he had the right to let me go, though I strongly hinted that if he exercised that right he might have some trouble getting along in Boston.

Would he have minded seeing me go? I don't know. I never knew what was going through that man's mind. I know he never indicated a strong desire to see me stay.

There was no controlling the guy. No way at all. The situation with John Y. was out of hand from the first moment he set foot in town. And it just grew worse as time went on.

He'd call all over the league, trying to pick the brains of other teams' coaches and GMs, then come running to me with all of these ideas which purportedly were his own. But I knew where they were coming from, because all of these people kept telling me what was going on. They'd call me up and ask, "Red, why's this guy bothering me?" After a while they got tired of his routine and figured, "I'll fix him." They began lying to him, feeding him bad information, giving him nothing but double-talk, and he never knew it. He never had a clue. He was too busy playing the big-shot owner.

Everyone knew there was a mounting strain between us, but publicly I wouldn't knock him. I'd say something like, "Well, he has his own ideas, and who knows, who's to say someone else's ideas might not be good ones, too? Let's find out. Let's give it a chance."

Ass-kissing? I'm sure it might have looked that way. God knows there were plenty of times I bit my tongue and said nothing; I couldn't even get innocuous statements out. But it wasn't ass-kissing at all. I simply didn't want the players—or the fans, for that matter—to feel there was dissension in the front office. Because that stuff spreads down. Once players start believing there's insecurity in the front office, they start playing for themselves and to hell with the team. They figure, "Hey, Red can't stop it if this guy wants to trade me," so they start playing with their bags packed and it affects the chemistry of your whole operation.

That's why I kept my mouth shut for as long as I could.

Many times owners want to become involved in the actual negotiations for players. They somehow get the idea that, whatever you might have signed a player for, they could have gotten him for less. That was like a red flag for me; it always made me mad. "You think it's

easy?" I'd say to the owner. "All right, you sign him."
Invariably, an owner ends up paying much more money
than was necessary. I'd had one owner who came to me
with his recommendation for an offer to a player. I
said, "I'll tell you what. You want to make that deal?
Fine, *you* make it. I don't want any part of it. The
responsibility will be yours, and I'm going to tell the
press that even though I work for you, I don't like it.
I'm not going to lie for you." He thought about that for
a moment, then backed off. I ended up signing the guy
for a hell of a lot less.

John Y. was one of those guys who fancied himself
as a real slick wheeler-dealer. He was also the best
example I've ever seen of a little knowledge being a
dangerous thing.

Take the Earl Tatum deal.

I said, "John, you're active on the phone"—I'm
figuring maybe I can get him off my back here—"why
don't you see if you can find us a backcourtman?" He
asked, "Who's available?" I said, "I hear Indiana's trying
to get rid of Earl Tatum. Maybe we could pick him up
for a late draft choice. If we move before they put him
on waivers, anything they get is a plus, so maybe they'll
go along with it."

I get a call from him later: "I think I can get
Tatum for a second-round pick? How's that sound?"

I said it sounded pretty good but that I wanted to
blow it by Satch Sanders—he was coaching for us
then—to see what he thought. Satch liked the idea, too,
so I told John to go ahead and make the deal.

He came back later on, laughing.

"Well, I did it."

"Did what?"

"Made the Tatum deal."

"What'd you give them?"

"I gave them $50,000 . . ."

I just looked at him. I couldn't believe it. There
wasn't any mention of money in our discussion.

"Then," he says, "we worked out something on a
draft choice, too."

Now I'm figuring maybe, because of the dough,

they agreed to a late-round choice, like third, fourth or even fifth.

"Yep," he says. "I gave 'em a first-round choice!"

I was horrified. "You didn't. You *couldn't* have done something like that."

"Yes, I did."

I wanted to hit him. "Look," I told him, "it's your ballclub, so you can do any goddamned thing you want with it. I can't stop you. But I want you to know, I don't like it. I don't like it at all."

I think that was the moment when I made up my mind that if he was going to own the team, I didn't want anything to do with it. That was in July 1978. He'd been with us only a couple of months, but I'd seen all I wanted to see.

When you give your life to something—and I'd given mine to the Celtics—you just don't get up and walk away from it lightly. Oh, there were times I could have left. Lots of them. Back when I retired from coaching, before Ted Turner bought the Hawks, Ted Cousins, the owner in Atlanta, offered me a five-year deal that included a piece of the franchise if I'd coach for him and become his GM. And there were plenty of other flattering offers. But before most of them were even on the table I'd say, "Look. Forget it. I'm not interested. There's no sense even discussing it."

The thought of leaving never really entered my mind, not even in the worst of times when some of our ownerships bled us dry. We were winning championships without a nickel in the bank. No one would ever believe how bad things got at times. We had airline companies shutting off our credit. One time I had to put up $9,000 of my own money in order to get the club onto a flight. When the phone company threatened to shut us down I personally visited the business office to ask for an extension of our credit. Embarrassing? You bet it was. It was an indignity we didn't deserve. But what could we do about it? There were times when we didn't even know who our owners were; all we knew was that we'd been purchased by some faceless corporation. Again. There were names on our payroll that I'd never heard of; everything was handled out of New York. During one of those ownerships a messenger arrived on the shuttle every Monday morning to pick up the gate receipts and bring them back to New York with him on the next shuttle. They took the money and never paid the bills. Believe me, we had some hard times, even while we were hanging all those flags.

Yet I never really thought of leaving. There was just something about the name *Celtics* that wouldn't let me go. And money had nothing to do with it. You simply can't buy what this team has given me over the years. It's like I've often pointed out, there are owners in sports today who'd gladly fork over millions of dollars to be able to wear a championship ring, but those rings aren't for sale. You can't buy them. You've got to earn them.

But John Y. Brown was more than I could take.

Sonny Werblin's a good friend of mine, and he'd always told me I could have a job with his organization anytime I wanted one. Now I wanted one. Or so I kept telling myself.

Mike Burke was retiring as president of basketball for the Madison Square Garden Corporation, and Sonny told me he wanted me to take the job. I was more than intrigued. New York and me? It would have been interesting. He said, "Red, I'll give you anything you want: Apartments, whatever." He was just super to me. I told him I wanted to think about it.

And I *did* think about it. My wife Dot was the first to get to me. "Arnold," she said, "if you're going to quit, then come home. Don't go to New York. I just can't imagine you *not* a Celtic."

I couldn't imagine it either.

Still, my mind wasn't really made up the morning I met my personal attorney, Bob Richards, and headed to Logan Airport for a flight to New York and another meeting with Werblin. I was going to give him my answer; I told him I would, and he was waiting to hear it.

I was walking to get a cab when I heard it the first time: *"Red! Don't go!"* It was some guy working on the street. Then I heard it again. And again. I must have heard it 20 times. Then the cabbie told me the same thing. As we walked onto the plane the pilot stopped me. Same thing: *"Don't go!"* I was touched. Bob was touched. It was a very emotional experience. They were all telling me what I already knew: I owed it to the team and I owed it to myself to give it one last shot in Boston.

That's what I told Sonny when we got to New York, and he was great about it. He's a class act. I like him, I respect him. I'd have had no problems at all working for him. I doubt that we spent more than 30 seconds discussing money; that was never the big issue from my point of view or his. Our discussions just centered on the job.

I came back to Boston and held a press conference. I said, "It wasn't a matter of money. It was just a matter of where I wanted to be." The headline in one of the papers the next morning read: THE PRIDE OF THE CELTICS: RED LET HIS HEART OVERRULE HIS HEAD.

No question about it, I did.

Things quieted down for a while, but with John Y. it was only a matter of time before the next bomb went off. The Earl Tatum thing really bothered me, but it couldn't hold a candle to the Bob McAdoo deal seven months later. That one took the cake.

We were having a terrible season. Havlicek was gone. The Archibald-Barnes-Knight thing never worked out. We ended up losing 53 games that year, the worst record in the history of our franchise. The Boston press was starting to climb all over Brown, and this really upset him; he was extremely sensitive to criticism.

We had a home-and-home series with the Knicks that February; down there Saturday night, back to our place Sunday afternoon. We won the Saturday game, and when we arrived home Sunday morning the papers were filled with rumors of a big trade involving McAdoo. Brown had gone to P. J. Clarke's with Sonny Werblin, and I guess he wanted to show everyone what a big wheel he was. That's what I figure he had bought the team for: The prestige, the ego gratification of being associated with the Celtics. Later on, word had it that it was his wife, Phyllis George, who came up with the bright idea of having McAdoo come to Boston. I don't know if that was true or not. All I know is that it wasn't my idea.

Sonny was smart. He went along with Brown: "Let's make a deal!" He wanted to get rid of McAdoo anyway, so he started bringing up the guy's stats. There they are, talking a big deal, and nobody's got any contracts in front of him so there's no way of verifying any of the essential information.

Brown calls me up. I tell him, "No way, I don't like it. I don't approve of it." All right, he finally agreed, no deal; he'd back off. I left the Garden that night believing it wouldn't happen.

But it did happen. The deal was officially announced the next morning; apparently it had been consummated over the phone the previous afternoon, sometime after Brown told me he wouldn't do it.

How crazy had the situation become? Get this: When Jan Volk, my legal aide who's now our general manager, got into the office that morning he began going over the paperwork and discovered there was a major issue involving $1 million of deferred compensation that had been assumed by the Knicks when they acquired McAdoo from Buffalo in 1976. Now it was up in the air as to whose responsibility that would become! When Jan brought this to Brown's attention, Brown told him, "Don't worry about that. You stay out of it; I'll take care if it."

Meanwhile, Brown's partner, Harry Mangurian, who kept a pretty low profile, called the office and wanted to know what the hell was going on. Jan told him about the $1 million question and also told him how Brown had ordered him to keep his nose out of it. Harry became very concerned and told Jan: "I don't care what *he* said; I want *you* to straighten that out."

It did get straightened out, and the obligation went back to the Knicks where it belonged. But if it had been left up to Brown—who was very poor on details—we'd have eaten that mistake.

That was it; that was enough for me. There was just no living with the situation any longer. The man was just so hyper, so adamant, so unwilling to listen to suggestions, so certain that he knew it all, when in reality he didn't know a damn thing about what he was doing.

So I put it right to him. "John," I said, "if you don't sell this team, I'm going to leave."

There had been rumors that he was thinking of selling to Mangurian, who, as his partner, had first option to purchase Brown's interest in the club. So I went to Harry, too. I told him if he didn't own the team within two weeks from that day, a Tuesday, I'd be gone.

Werblin had told me he'd keep that job offer alive for three years, a great gesture on his part. But I made up my mind that I wasn't going to jerk him around again. Therefore, I was very firm in my remarks to Mangurian. "Harry," I told him, "you're a nice guy, a good businessman. I'd have no trouble working for you. But I'm not interested in offers that have been tendered or any of that crap. Those things can be kicked around for months, and meanwhile I'm still dealing with John Y. So as far as I'm concerned, if you don't own this team outright—that means 100 percent—two weeks from now, then you can count me out. I don't want to be here. You can run it yourself. I'm not going to sit around cooling my heels while lawyers go through tons of paper. I won't hang around for that. I'll release myself from the situation."

Well, it took two weeks, but Harry did it. He bought out John Y. Brown. Ten weeks later we signed Larry Bird, whom I'd drafted the previous spring as a junior eligible at Indiana State, and two years after that we were world champions again.

The nine-month siege was over. That's how long Brown owned the Celtics. Nine months. But it was long enough to nearly destroy what we'd spent 30 years putting together. And you wonder why I say a little knowledge is a dangerous thing?

Harry Mangurian owned the Celtics for four years:

Four great years, including a championship in 1981. Then he sold the franchise to Don Gaston, Alan Cohen and Paul Dupee, who began their ownership with the 1984 championship and still own us today.

I've always believed good organization begins at the top. That's where the real strength is, and it filters down from there. We're in good hands today. And, believe me, no one appreciates that any more than I do.

6.

Beware, the Agents Cometh

"Boy, how they scheme!"

It's funny how images work. You never see yourself the way others see you. I'm thought of as a very tough, hard-fisted negotiator who's always at war with the agents. But that's not true; at least I don't think it is.

It's just that there are certain things I believe in, and I think I've shown the patience and guts to stand up for them. I'm not the kind of guy who easily capitulates, and I make no apology for it.

When Larry Bird signed his last contract, for instance, reporters were expecting a terrific battle because everyone knew that Larry had his eyes set upon becoming one of the highest-paid players in the game, and rightly so.

They wanted to know what my strategy would be; here's what I told them. You could look it up; it was in the papers well before negotiations got started. "Normally, when you negotiate with an agent you look to a player's faults," I said. "You begin by saying, 'He's a damn good player, but . . .' It might be, 'but he doesn't play strong defense.' Or, 'but he doesn't box out.' Whatever. But with Larry there are no buts. What can you say? He's team-oriented, he plays hurt, and all he wants to do is win. He's all heart and he's fulfilled everything we ever expected of him. I wish *I* was his agent! There's simply no case to be made against that kid."

I'm interested in happy players and I try to be reasonable, but a reasonable negotiation has to be a two-way street. I've done a lot of complaining about agents and with good cause, because there are a lot of unsavory ones out there.

What separates the good ones from the bad ones? Many things, but most of all, the good ones really have the best interests of their clients at heart.

If you're a kid coming out of school with a tremendous future, how do you know which one to pick? I wish there was an easy answer. So many factors enter into it. The first thing I'd recommend is to get an adviser to help in the selection. It might be a parent, a coach, maybe a minister. But even that's no guarantee. Agents have been known to go right to the preacher or the mother and father and sell them a bill of goods; it's really the same old game that was played when the kid was recruited for college. And coaches have sometimes been known to receive a little payoff for steering a player in the direction of a certain agent; it's like a commission, you know what I mean? Oh yes, it happens. Some agents even get guys already in the pros to go out and solicit more clients; then those guys get a piece of the action, too.

And they scheme. Boy, how they scheme! More than a few have been known to advance money to kids while they're still in college so that the kids will feel obliged to hire them as their representatives. That's one thing I'd tell any kid unequivocally: *Don't accept a loan from any agent while you're still in school!* No matter how much you might need the money. They'll come up to the kid and say, "Hey, wouldn't you like to be driving a Cadillac or a Mercedes? Don't you want to buy a home for your mother? Why wait until later on? I'll advance you some money now and you can pay me back out of your contract ..." That's how they get their foot in the door. I make them sound like whores, huh? Too bad. A lot of them are. Hell, I can't be quoted on specific situations, but there have been athletes who—while still in college—have owed agents as much as $150,000, and I know their names. It happens, especially in football.

A kid that good doesn't have to take money like that. He can borrow from a bank based on his future earnings; he doesn't have to get involved in a shady commitment to anyone.

I wish there was a way to weed out these ambulance chasers, but I'm not sure how it could be done. The NFL has a good idea: It registers agents who want to represent football players. They attend a seminar and pay some dues and then get this card which authorizes them to negotiate on behalf of their clients. If they aren't registered, no football team will talk with them. As far as I know, that rule has never been challenged. It's a step in the right direction—though, really, it's only a minor deterrent. If they won't see such-and-such a guy, what's he do? He gets another agent to join him and they split the deal. Or, if he thinks he's got a chance at grabbing a really good prospect, he joins the association. And if they try to stop him, they've got a big lawsuit on their hands. It's one thing to *think* a guy's a bum, a real seedy character, but if you're going to say it and publicly malign his professional reputation, you'd damn well better be able to prove it or your butt's headed for court. You start arbitrarily excluding people and you'll be in lawsuits up to your ears.

What it comes down to, really, is that you have *no* control over who's going to represent a kid. And after you've seen enough of them abused or taken for a sleigh ride—I mean really having their naiveté exploited—it's difficult not to feel a bit contemptuous when you find yourself sitting across a desk from one of these birds. After a while you know who the good ones are, and you respect them. You know who the other ones are, too.

Even if an agent is also an attorney, I would expect him—after having negotiated the best contract he possibly could—to take his client over to a bank or to a reputable investment house like E.F. Hutton or Paine, Webber or L.F. Rothschild, one of those, and say: "Here's a man who has so much income. I would like to have him put on a budget, and I would like somebody to handle his money so that his taxes will be taken care of and he'll have a portfolio of sound investments."

If a guy's making big money, he should pay his taxes and then have expert counseling as to the kinds of investments that will provide him with an income for the rest of his life, long after his playing days are over.

There are at least two or three guys in the NBA right now—I'm talking about guys in the $1 million a year category—who don't have a dime! Their investments have all gone sour, which means they've got to pay back Uncle Sam, and now they're on the hook for big money.

This is a big, big problem, and I lay it largely at the feet of some of these damn agents who take it upon themselves to act as investment counselors when they have no business wearing that hat. And I blame them, not their kids. What's a kid supposed to know? He's got to trust someone, doesn't he? So he trusts his agent. Meanwhile he's busy writing checks and the money has no meaning to him. It's just a number in a book, and with each check it dwindles a bit, but who cares? There's plenty more in the bank. Let's have a party! Let's have some fun! He forgets all about his taxes and his other obligations. He doesn't know what's happening until one day he finds Uncle Sam breathing down his back and he looks into his pockets and discovers that he's broke. The agent? He's nowhere to be found. He's long gone, looking for another pigeon.

This is even more of a problem in those sports where the kids have never been through college. They have no idea what to do with their money. At least most basketball players have been exposed to higher education, though that doesn't stop a lot of them from getting burned. Burned? Hell, scorched!

Some of these agents, they not only invest in deals for their clients—but they receive a commission for doing so, too; so they're making it on both ends. They'll get the kid to buy into a deal, get a little piece for themselves on the side, and then charge the kid for having engineered the whole thing. If you're getting paid both ways, you don't have to be quite so concerned about whether it's a totally safe investment, do you?

They keep telling these kids, "Invest your money in depreciation real estate. Don't pay taxes. You don't have to pay them." So the kid doesn't pay taxes because he's got all these write-offs—but then comes Judgment Day, when the apartments, or whatever they are, stop working in his favor. All of a sudden his investments are no good.

There are so many variations to the theme, but the bottom line is always the same: The kid ends up the loser. So when they ask me, I tell them they're better off taking that money, paying their taxes until they get a little bit older and more knowledgeable about these things, and entrusting the rest to a reputable bank or investment house who'll handle it professionally for them.

The kids who listen to the agents who say, "I'll invest it for you," are usually the kids who wind up without a nickel to their names. And the sad part is, it's hard to blame them. They just don't know any better. They simply place their faith in the wrong guy. And there are an awful lot of wrong guys out there on the prowl.

If you think agents are unscrupulous when it comes to investments, you ought to see them at the bargaining table.

Again, some of them do a great job for their clients. I particularly admire the ones who keep up their interest after their kids have been fired or let go by the teams they were playing for in the pros. These agents will try to find jobs for them or maybe place them with clubs over in Europe, things like that. The point is, they really *care*.

But there are too many who don't care about anything or anyone; all they care about is lining their own damn pockets. Many times you'll see an agent sign a kid to a long-term deal in order to get his percentage fattened when he knows—or *should* know, assuming he's got a brain in his head—that it would be in the kid's best interest to sign for a shorter period of time. But you see, their fear is that at the end of a short-term deal the kid might decide to change agents and they'll lose out. So they tie him up.

Here's how it works. Let's say the kid's going to make $1 million a year over three years. The agent's going to take five percent of that, or $150,000. But if he can stretch out the terms to five years, his take jumps up to $250,000. Well, suppose at the end of three years the kid wises up and says, "Hey, you've done nothing for me. All you're doing is taking my money. What have you gotten me in all this time? Who needs you? I'm dumping you and finding somebody who knows what's going on."

If that happens, the agent's out his extra $100,000. So, planning ahead, he signs the kid to a five-year deal instead of three, telling him it's for his benefit when, in reality, it's strictly for the agent's benefit.

This is one of the most obvious areas where you can separate the good agents from the shysters. The good ones are content and satisfied to collect a normal commission based on what they believe is best for their clients. If they really think a five-year deal is practical, fine; they go for it. But if not, they'll say to the kid: "Look, why not go for three? You're coming into the peak of your career. The only thing we'd be gambling on is that you don't get hurt, and we can take out a policy to cover us there. If we do that, we might be in a lot better negotiating position three years from now."

The first thing I try to do when they come into my office, if I don't know who I'm dealing with, is size them up, get a feel for where they're coming from, try to figure out in my own mind if they're strictly on the level or out to make a killing. After you've been doing it for a while, you become pretty good at picking out the phonies.

Sometimes a new guy will surprise you. He'll be almost humble when he begins: "Look, Red, I'll admit I don't know too much about this, so all I can go by is what some of the other people in the league are getting. I feel my guy has to be at least within that range . . ."

I don't have any problems with an approach like that; I want happy players, too. If both sides are reasonable, something can be worked out. But, as a rule, all of these guys are "experts" the minute they walk into your office, and you can bet your life the first thing out of their mouths is going to be stats, stats, stats.

It makes you laugh. They haven't seen the kid play more than two or three times, but now they presume they're going to sit down with a professional GM and try to convince him how good this player is, what he can do for the ballclub, and so on.

They don't know what the hell they're talking about, yet many times they get away with it. They actually fool some GMs! How do they do it? They study the statistics and study the amounts of money being paid to players of comparable ability. Of course, they never take into account all of the things that you'll never define by statistics, and they *never* talk about players of comparable ability who might be getting less.

All right, I understand that everybody has to start somewhere, so you've got to be a little bit patient at first. If the agent sitting in front of you doesn't have any credentials, doesn't have a proven track record, you still give him the benefit of the doubt when the initial meeting begins. I say *initial* because no matter what you offer an agent in the beginning, he'll never take it. He wants to show his client that he's earning his dough, so if you're talking about a player of any consequence you have to figure on having at least three or four meetings. That's almost standard now.

So the guy starts off by giving you the amount he's after.

"Wait a minute," I tell him. "Where'd you get that figure from?"

"Well," he says, "I understand that so-and-so's getting this much, and my guy's as good as he is . . ."

Now you know where his head's at. He has no idea about the economics of the business. He doesn't know that some teams make money and other teams lose money; some lose money even while selling out their building every night, and they just can't afford to pay what other teams are paying.

But he doesn't want to know about all of that. He's not interested in any other facet of the industry. All he knows is that so-and-so is making X number of dollars and somebody told him his client is every bit as good, therefore that's what he wants. End of discussion.

And naturally he hasn't tried to figure out what his kid's actual contribution is. I mean *beyond* the stats. Not a word about chemistry or performance in the clutch or producing under pressure. Nothing. Just stats.

Well, I always had a rule about stats, and all of my players knew it. I never wanted anyone bringing his statistics with him when he came in to discuss his contract. I didn't want to see them or even hear about them. Why? Because I never believed in them.

A lot of statisticians cheat on things like rebounds and assists, trying to build up reputations for their own guys. So what good are numbers when you've got crap like that going on? What's a steal? What's an assist? If a guy gets a rebound and then hands it to another guy who dribbles down the floor and makes a basket, does that mean the first guy gets an assist? Not in my mind. But it's been known to happen.

There's only one true statistic, and that's free-throw shooting. The rest of them are much too vague, much too subject to interpretation and prejudice to be of any use in telling you what you really want to know. So I'd tell my guys: "Your salary depends on what I've seen with my own two eyes. Until the day your statistics can tell me how many points were scored in the clutch and how many came in garbage time, I don't want to see them."

No Celtic has ever been paid according to how many points, rebounds, steals, assists or any other totals he might have compiled. Each man gets paid according to how well he does what we've asked him to do. What was his contribution to making us a better team? That's the only thing I ever cared about. In our system the guy who set the good pick was just as important as the guy who made the jump shot. Take people like Satch Sanders and KC Jones, probably the best defensive players we've ever had. If they could stop Elgin Baylor and Jerry West from getting their normal number of points, wasn't that worth as much to us as if they both scored 20 while letting Jerry and Elgin toss in 100? See what I mean? There were plenty of nights when their great defense helped us win important games, yet what stat would ever tell you that? What numbers were they supposed to bring in at contract time? They had none. Yet they were two of our most essential players on the court.

So whenever a new agent started off his conversation with me by bringing up his client's statistics, I'd set him straight right away. That wasn't the way we played basketball in Boston. Once that foolishness was out of the way and the ground rules had been established, we could get down to basics.

Anybody can represent the Birds, the Olajuwons, the Jordans, the Bowies, the guys who go one-two-three at the top of the draft. There's not much room for dispute at that level. But later on in the first round, and down into the second round, where you're hunting to get a kid a job, that's where an agent really earns his fee. And this is where the games are played.

Everybody's different. Every situation is different. Personally, I don't like a situation where I say, "Here, I'll give your guy $50,000," and the agent says, "No, we want $500,000," when you both know you're going to settle somewhere in the neighborhood of $250,000. I don't want to go through all of that hassling. It's ludicrous. It always ends up in a yelling match.

So I usually come in with a figure I'm going to stick to, or one very close to it. If I know a player's worth $300,000, I might come in at $250,000 or $275,000, so I'll have a little leeway if I think it becomes necessary. Otherwise, I'll stick to my original offer.

But now the agent figures I'm like some of the other guys he's dealt with. I tell him right up front: "Your guy's worth about $250,000, so don't go telling me he's worth $1 million, figuring that might boost my offer to $600,000. It doesn't work that way with me."

That's their favorite trick. They'll want $750,000, so they start out demanding $1.5 million while you're offering $400,000, hoping eventually you'll get tired and agree to split the difference, which means they walk out with $900,000 or whatever it is. As soon as they start that stuff I tell them, "Okay, buster, if that's the way you plan to negotiate, I'm going to start off at $50,000 and let you sweat your way up to $300,000, which is what we should have been talking about anyway!"

The other great trick they have is coming after you with perks: Little frills and bonuses over and above the basic compensation. They'll agree with you on a nice salary; let's say, $750,000. Then they'll say, "If my guy decides to go back to college, you pay his tuition." Or pay for his trips back home; whatever it might be.

Or one of their favorites: "We want an extra $10,000 if he makes the all-star team." That one really steams me. "Look," I tell them, "if I pay him $750,000 and he *doesn't* make the all-star team, I've got to be an idiot!"

They all play that game, nickel-and-diming you to death if you let them get away with it. We've been fortunate in Boston. No Celtic has any perks. Oh, once in a while you get a player in a trade who's got a perk or two from a previous contract. But there are no perks in the contracts we give our guys. I tell them: "All I want to know is what it will cost us to have you play basketball for the Boston Celtics. We are not in the real estate business. We are not in the travel business. We are not in the automobile business. All we're in is the basketball business. So what will it cost us for you to play basketball? That's all we're interested in. Make your own investments. Buy your own cars. Get your own deals with the bank. Buy your own tickets home. If this stuff really bothers you, then let's translate it into dollars right now.'

It gets ridiculous. A guy making $1 million in salary, plus another $200,000 on a sneaker endorsement, plus whatever he gets from commercials and appearances, is sitting there asking you to give him another $2,000 if he decides he wants to go to school!

Sometimes that perk stuff backfires on them. It did in the Paul Westphal case a little while back. Phoenix signed him as a free agent just before the 1983–84 season began. He was supposed to get something like an extra $250,000 if he appeared in 60 games that year. Well, he appeared in 59, although he was *available* to have played in 61. It so happened that his coach, John MacLeod, chose not to use him on two occasions. Now Westphal and his agent are all upset and decide they're going to take formal action against the Suns. They did, and they lost the decision. In my mind, that was a correct ruling. See, what they ended up doing was outsmarting themselves. If they had worded the perk correctly—specifying how many games Paul was *available* to play in, rather than how many he actually played—they would have been able to pocket the dough.

What do you end up with in a situation like that? A player who has hard feelings, even though MacLeod might have been perfectly right, from a coaching standpoint, not to have used him on those two occasions.

That's one good example—and I can think of many—of why we stay away from perks. A guy is paid to do a job and that's it. No strings attached.

When we've completed a contract negotiation with one of our players, and he's sitting there across from me with his agent, we have a standard conversation that goes something like this:

"Do you like this contract?"

"It's fine. Very fine. We're quite satisfied."

"Good. I'm satisfied, too. What about the length of it? Are you happy with that as well?"

"Yes. No problem."

"Great. That means if you have a good year next season, or the season after, I'm not going to expect to see you back here asking me to renegotiate this deal, right?"

"That's right."

"Good. Because I won't do it. Not even if it costs me my own job."

Then I lay it out in even more specific terms:

"Here's the way I see it. If you go out and have a super season, and all of a sudden there are now players of lesser ability in this league who are making more than you are, that's my plus. Your plus is that you've got a security blanket of guaranteed money for the life of this contract. If you don't have a good year, you get paid. If you are plagued by pesky injuries, you get paid. If you suffer a permanent injury, you get paid. If you're in an automobile accident, you get paid. Those are your pluses.

"So, you have your pluses and I have my plus—but my only plus is that maybe, if you play very well, I might have you for a little bit less than you're actually worth. That's the gamble you're taking. Meanwhile, I'm taking all of these other gambles.

"So, if we're in agreement on all of these things, let's sign the contract. If we're not, we've got to figure out something else. Because that's the only way I'm going to enter into this agreement with you, and I want it clearly understood right now."

I know of a case where a player signed a long-term contract, then went out that first year and had a hell of a season; so he asked management to renegotiate the deal. Well, the team didn't want to, but it felt forced to because he'd become an all-star player. Next year, same damn thing happened. He wanted to renegotiate again, and the team capitulated again. Then he went in a *third* time the following season, but now the club put its foot down. Nothing doing. So he said, "Ouch, I just hurt my back."

What did the team do? It figured for another $50,000 or $100,000 it could make his back well in a hurry, so again it capitulated.

What would I have done? It's difficult to speak for someone else's problems, especially when they involve a player as important as this guy was. Nevertheless, I'd have put him and his "bad back" into a hospital immediately. Bad back? Let's see. And then have the doctors stick him so full of goddamned needles he'd think he was a pincushion! That might change his mind in a hurry. And, of course, if they discovered there was nothing wrong with his back, you might have a pretty good case against him.

I wouldn't accuse him of faking it, mind you. I'd just tell him, as I walked away from his bedside, "I want you to *stay* here until you're all better. When you're ready to play you can put your clothes on."

7.

Basketball and Fun

"It's also a game that can drive you nuts."

The first formal coaching job I ever had was at St. Albans Prep, a very high-class school in Washington. I took it while I was going for my Master's degree at George Washington.

For four or five days I went through all kinds of thoughts and theories; then I put the kids through a scrimmage and realized that everything I had been telling them was way over their heads. It was a young team, made up of mostly freshmen and sophomores. I still see some of them from time to time and we kid about this.

One of the guys I really like to kid is Jim Simpson of ESPN. He was a student at the school and couldn't make the team. Then, at my next job, Roosevelt High in Washington, I pulled this big kid out of the hallways and talked him into coming out for basketball. I later had to cut him. His name was Bowie Kuhn. Small world, huh?

Anyway, when I saw that no one was absorbing any of my wisdom at St. Albans, I blew my whistle and stopped the scrimmage. "Everyone come over here," I said. "Okay, listen up. I want you to drive from your minds everything I've taught you these past few days. We're going to start all over . . ."

Then I reached for a ball and held it up so that everyone could see it. "Gentlemen," I said, "this is a basketball. The object of this game is to take this ball and stick it into that hole over there. Then you must all get together as a team and make sure the other team doesn't stick this same ball into this hole over here . . ." And we went from there.

It taught them a lesson, I think, and it taught me a lesson, too. Basketball is a very simple game. So why complicate it?

I see what some teams are doing and it makes me laugh. You can hire all the specialists you want: A coach to teach the centers, a coach to teach the forwards, a psychologist, a psychiatrist, a weight-lifter, a conditioner, a nutritionist, and right on down the line. Yet the purpose of the game remains the same: *to take a round object and throw it into a hole!* All of this other crap isn't needed.

Okay, today aerobics is the big thing. Everyone warms up to music. Hey, the Celtics do it, too. That's fine. That's progress. I have no problem with that— though I've often kidded to friends that I'm not sure I could coach effectively today, because I've never run a video cassette recorder and I'm not up on rock music.

But let me give you an example of the kind of stuff I'm talking about. I once got a letter from a psychiatrist, who followed it up with a phone call, telling me he felt he could make a large contribution to motivating our team. Plus, he said, he wanted to be affiliated with the Celtics. I told him, "You've got to be a jerk." This upset him. "No, really," I said, "think about it. We've won six championships in a row, right? Now how are you going to motivate a team to do better than that? Can you win *seven* championships in six years? This is not ego on my part; it's stupidity on your part! Why don't you call up a team that's *not* winning? Goodbye."

It's a simple game. You don't need all this other baloney.

It's also a game of fun. Even at the pro level, I've always believed that basketball should remain a game of fun. Sure, there's a lot of conditioning and discipline involved in it, too, but basically it's still a game of fun. Why is it fun? Because there's no other game in history that people play for pure enjoyment as much as they play basketball. You'll find it on every playground: One-on-one, two-on-two, or maybe just a kid killing hours with his jump shot. You won't find that in baseball, football or any other sport.

So why take away the fun aspect just because you're now playing in a disciplined situation? You can have fun and still be disciplined.

Oh, sure, sometimes you have to do crazy things to get your point across. Sometimes you try to make your players mad. I remember one night when Kentucky won a game in Madison Square Garden but looked so bad winning it that Adolph Rupp waited for everyone to leave the building, then had the lights turned on again and started a practice at midnight.

It's also a game that can drive you nuts, because you're always at the mercy of things you can't control. No matter what you do or how well you prepare, how well you scout, how well you motivate, you *can't* score from the bench. All I could do as a coach was direct. I used to tell my players this all the time: "Look, we can work the best play, execute it the best way, with everyone doing his job, with perfect timing"—I was a great believer in timing—"and after doing all of that, someone could blow a layup or miss a shot. So you've always got to be ready and prepared to adjust."

To me, it's the superior sport, played by the superior athletes.

Football's an extremely rigid game where most guys operate in a limited area of assignment. If you're a tackle, you do this; if you're a guard, you do that. When the defense has the ball, you sit on your butt and do nothing. When you have the ball, you still get to rest 30 seconds between each play. And did you ever watch them working out in camp? They push a sled up and down the field. That's fun?

Hockey? They're all little guys. Once in a while they get a big guy and they make him a defenseman. It's a game that's played exclusively on the ground. All you need is a stocky little guy with good legs and strong wrists. The whole human race is getting bigger, but in hockey the players have got to remain small because their game is played on the floor.

Baseball people always amaze me. They live in the past. Spring training: Sure, I can see going to Florida where the weather's warm, but what's this crap about bringing the wife and kids and your golf clubs? I've heard of ballplayers singing in nightclubs during spring training. Believe me, no Celtic ever felt like singing after a day at one of our camps. I used to discuss baseball with Lou Boudreau all the time when he managed the Red Sox. You know, he was a great basketball player in his day; really, a good one. When he came up with that famous shift against Ted Williams, back when he managed the Indians before he came to Boston, I thought it was a fabulous idea. You hardly ever see innovations like that in baseball.

I used to tell him, "Lou, instead of pulling righthanders out for lefthanders and all of that stuff, if you've got a real good pitcher in there and he's throwing well, why not stick him on first until you need him again, rather than losing him for the rest of the game? Why not play the percentages?" See, that's what I'd have done if I'd managed a baseball team. Why does a pitcher have to pitch nine innings? Why wait until his arm gets tired? Why not have him pitch three innings, then pull him out of there, just like they do in an all-star game? That way you can bring him back the next day. Why not manage every game as if it were an all-star game? That way you'd get used to use your ace much more often.

The answer was always, "We don't do things like that in baseball." Which, to me, was no answer at all.

It reminds me of the time I was driving to an exhibition game with Gene Conley. Gene, to the best of my knowledge, is still the only man to have earned championship rings in two professional sports. He backed up Russell for three years as a reserve center—a damn good one—and pitched for several big league teams, including the Milwaukee Braves when they won the World Series.

We've got the World Series on the radio. Early Wynn's pitching for Chicago. He's their ace pitcher, and now they jump out to something like a quick 9–0 lead.

"Take him out!" I said. "It's cold and he's old. He could get hurt. Take him out now and you can bring him back tomorrow."

"Can't do it," Conley said.

"Why can't you?"

"He's gotta go five to get the win."

"You're kidding me! To hell with the win. Let's win the goddamn Series." I couldn't believe it.

Now five innings go by.

"Okay," I said, "he's got the win. Take him out."

"Can't, Red."

"Now why?"

"He's got a shutout going."

Well, he won his game. Big deal. He also hurt his arm and didn't win another game the rest of the Series, which only strengthened my belief that statistics don't mean a damn thing. The only thing that matters is winning.

That's the problem with baseball. Nobody wants to try anything new because they're so caught up in traditions and statistics.

I'll take basketball over any game that's ever been played. Of the four major team sports it's the only one that's truly a natural sport. In baseball you've got special equipment: Gloves and bats. In hockey you've got pads, skates and a stick. In football your helmet is a weapon, and your whole body's wrapped up in padding. In all these games you're using equipment you weren't born with.

Okay, you weren't born with sneakers either. But you *could* play our game barefooted; they certainly do in a lot of places. You've got no pads, no artificial help; there's complete freedom of movement.

In baseball the first baseman's mitt has improved so much over the years that today's fielders have to be better than the ones who played years ago with thin little gloves that barely covered their hands. And remember the old leather helmets in football? You had to run a different way back then. Now, as soon as a runner sees trouble, he ducks his head and comes at you with this tremendous weapon.

But in basketball you have none of these artificial helpmates. You have continuous motion. You have eye–hand coordination. And you have touch. You can play it on the ground or play it in the air, and it brings in all phases of running: Backward, forward, sideward. You start and you stop, then you start again. The main thing is continuous motion.

Hockey has continuous motion, but you're on skates and you have an artificial propulsion. In football you rest between each play. In baseball you run only when the ball is hit to you or when you hit the ball. And even then, you're just running to a base where you stop. Other than that, you could be standing in left field doing nothing for 30 minutes.

Basketball combines more facets of skill than any other sport. You could be a tremendous power in the line in football, yet all you've got to do is run eight feet. Then you rest. Sure, there's body contact; I understand all of that. But the basketball player's got to run, jump, react, be ambidextrous and creative, and all the while remain in continuous motion.

There's no other game like that.

People are always coming up with gimmicks to improve the game. Someone once suggested: "Why don't you practice with heavy sneakers so that your guys will feel faster when they put on the lighter ones for games?" I told him, "Right. That makes a lot of sense—about as much as the story of the guy who kept hitting himself on the head with a hammer because it felt so good when he stopped."

Someone else came up with the idea of a gadget you attach to the rim so that the ball can't fall through.

This was supposed to be used in rebounding drills. It made no sense to me, because they wouldn't be *true* rebounds. You develop rebounding skills through instincts, through continual association with game situations. When a shot is taken from the right side, the percentages say that it's going to land in a certain place and you react accordingly. But these are instincts which can be learned only through experience. That's what made Russell the greatest rebounder who ever lived—and don't give me any of that crap about Chamberlain's statistics. Those are just numbers. When the game was on the line and the ball was up for grabs, Russell had no equal. He reduced rebounding to a science. In fact, he was the one who pointed out to me, "Timing and positioning are everything, because 80 percent of all rebounds are taken *below* the rim." He was always thinking, and he always knew exactly what he was doing.

Then there was that period when different teams tried wearing those psychedelic uniforms with the shirttails hanging out. You'll notice our uniforms haven't changed in 35 years, but some shrinks convinced some teams that this would make them play better. Ridiculous. Everybody's getting into the act. These same people are always pushing to put the players through various kinds of tests. My answer to that was: "Absolutely not! I don't want my players scared and I don't want them being used as guinea pigs. *I'll* be their psychologist. *I'll* be their psychiatrist. I don't need people coming in from the outside, people who have no feel whatsoever for what's happening on that court, hanging around our locker room and talking with authority about a game they don't understand at all."

You wouldn't believe the letters we get from chiropractors, osteopaths, the whole bunch of them, assuring us they can make us a better basketball team. I tell them all, "Thanks, but we've got a doctor. We'll call you if we need you."

I'll tell you another thing I don't like today: Cheerleaders. You don't need them at the professional level. They don't contribute anything. They're nothing more than a poor attempt to emulate the freshness of the college atmosphere. Whether it's football or basketball, they don't belong at the professional level, and I've been fighting that for years. They belong in high school. They belong in college. They *don't* belong in the professional game.

First, you've got enough problems in basketball without having girls hanging around the gym. Before you know it, they're making eyes at some of the guys, and some of the guys are going to stray. It happens.

But the main point is, they're running up and down the court, cheering their brains out, and nobody's cheering along with them. All they're really doing is entertaining themselves. You can't take professional fans to a pep rally, like they do in college, and hand out leaflets telling them: "These are the songs, and these are the cheers, so memorize them; then, when we bang the thing and have the horn, you come in and do this . . ."

It can't be done. So the idea of cheerleading is a facade, a joke, just an excuse to have some scantily clad girls running around, turning your game into a Broadway show. I don't like it. And I don't like cheerleading organists, either.

I'd much rather have high school tumblers and gymnasts doing routines for the crowd's enjoyment. And I *love* that double-dutch jump-roping kids are doing now. Of all the entertainments you see at basketball games today, that's my favorite.

You'll find jealousies in the game today; there's a lot of jealousy in sports.

When you win, people are always trying to knock you down. They don't want to copy you. They don't want to emulate you. They want to *destroy* you. That's why it's taken so many organizations such a long time to develop a winner. They didn't want to admit there were different ways to build a winning ballclub. They didn't want to do what we were doing. They wanted to show that they could beat us by doing what they'd been doing, even though they'd been doing it unsuccessfully for years.

I could never understand that. I've always felt that if a guy has something good, copy it! If I saw something I liked while watching a college game, something that made me think, Jeez, that might work real well with our personnel, you can bet I'd take it to practice with me and have our guys work on it. Why not? You've got to be open to new ideas.

The jealousies really show when it comes to voting for awards.

Take the Coach of the Year for 1983–84. Okay, Frank Layden might have been deserving of it, but my guy, KC Jones, *had* to be a close second. Utah went nowhere. It won its division, then got knocked out of the playoffs in the second round. Here we were, in the toughest division of all, with Philly, New York and Washington, and we win it by 10 games with a team that had been eliminated from the previous year's playoffs in four sraight! Plus, we go on to win the championship. So where does KC finish in the voting? Fourth. Behind Layden, Chuck Daly and Hubie Brown. No disrespect to those other guys, but that's a joke.

It becomes a popularity contest, plus you've got some people who figure, "Oh, Boston's won enough; let's spread it around."

You also have people who'll look for reasons why you should *not* get accolades, and that's wrong, too. When you win a championship, everyone's gunning for you.

Take Billy Cunningham in 1982–83. His club went 65–17 and won the championship, which means he had those guys up and motivated every single night. There's no possible way anyone could have coached any better than Billy did that season. He did a fabulous job. So where did he finish in the voting? Third. Behind Don Nelson, whose Bucks went 51–31 and lost in the conference finals, and Cotton Fitzsimmons, whose Kansas City team finished *third* in the Midwest Division and didn't even make the playoffs!

That's totally ludicrous. Instead of honoring a guy who did a magnificent job, they look at a guy like Fitzsimmons and say: "He finished third when he should have finished fifth, so let's give it to him." See, what they're really doing is looking for ways to discredit the success Cunningham had in Philadelphia, and that's not right.

But this happens all the time, in all sports. A guy is supposed to come in fourth, but he comes in second. Big deal. What about the guy who kept his team fired up, who met all of the big challenges and walked away with a flag? Doesn't that count for anything?

KC fourth? Billy third? You've got to be kidding.

But the biggest joke of all was when they picked the "best team ever" in conjunction with the league's 25th anniversary. They could have picked any one of the great Russell clubs that won eight championships in a row. Or else they could have picked the 1972–73 Lakers team that won 33 in a row. But no, they gave it to the 1966–67 Philadelphia team, a team that won *one* championship, a team Russell and the rest of our guys came back to eliminate the next two years in a row.

The truth is, they just didn't want to make the Silver Anniversary celebration into a Boston Celtics affair, regardless of the fact we probably deserved it. The thinking was, "Let's spread it around."

In my mind, that's small thinking.

The future of our game? I think it's bright. Oh sure, if the TV bubble ever bursts we're *all* going down the drain, every sport, because we're all at the mercy of TV now.

I think the one thing we need, more than anything else, is educated, enlightened owners who'll pass rules and make decisions with the good of the game foremost in their minds.

The only time I ever had real apprehensions about the future of the NBA was back when salaries seemed to jump out of sight overnight. That's when the other league was still in business, forcing us to bid big money for top players. Our whole salary structure fell out of line and I wasn't sure where it would end, or if we'd survive the tremendous obligations we were taking on. I had real misgivings then.

I can remember talking about it with my friend Dick O'Connell, who was general manager of the Red Sox at the time. He said, "You guys are crazy, giving them that kind of money."

The baseball people laughed at us. The hockey people laughed. The football people were practically hysterical. And I'd say, "Yeh, Dick, but just wait. Your turn will come."

"Sure, sure," he'd say, as if I were nuts.

But their turn did come. O'Connell called me up one day after he'd just had a session with a player and his agent who were looking for some pretty serious dough.

"Red," he said. "What the hell am I going to do?"

Now it was my turn to laugh, and I did. "Take two and hit to right," I told him. "That's what the hell you do."

8.

Lonesome in the Limelight

"I'd rather have a good pastrami."

Most people in the public eye are basically lonely; I know I was. They have a very small circle of friends with whom they can really unwind, really relax, really feel normal.

I remember how bad I used to feel for Ted Williams when he was in Boston. He was such a visible guy, with his face and his mannerisms and all of that, and he couldn't go anywhere without being harrassed, bothered, hit with all kinds of annoying questions. It was terrible. He might have been the most visible man in the city at the height of his career, and as a result he probably ate 90 percent of his meals in his room. The other 10 percent he'd eat off in a corner of some restaurant after practically sneaking in. He paid the price of fame, and, boy, it can be a high price. I suspect that, more than anything else, had a lot to do with him becoming such a private guy and getting all caught up in hunting and fishing.

You lose all semblance of privacy when you become a public figure, and the demands on your time just never end. Take a guy like John Havlicek. Who

112

ever had a sweeter disposition than that kid? He'd sign autographs by the hundreds, but then finally he'd have to say, "I've got to go now. I've got a plane to catch." What happens at that point? To the people left waiting in line he becomes a louse. See what I mean? Where does it end? Where is the end of how nice these guys are supposed to be?

That's why they end up becoming very private people, carefully selecting the few friends they'll allow themselves to get close to.

You become distrustful of people you meet. It's almost a form of paranoia: *Why is this guy being so friendly to me? Does he actually like me? Is there a possibility of a real friendship here? Or is he trying to get close because of who I am?* It's like the old expression: Beware of Greeks bearing gifts. No offense to Greeks; it's just a saying. But this is how you end up thinking once you're cast into the limelight.

The great athletes, the smart ones, become very hard to get close to. They don't take to people right away just because some guy reaches for the check. Or because the restaurant owner comes over and says, "Hey, put your money away; this one's on me."

That used to happen to me all the time. Back in the days when we couldn't sell tickets, before there was any TV money, salaries were largely dependent upon how well we did at the gate. I'd go to a restaurant, pay my check, and the guy would say: "How about a couple of tickets to the game?" I'd blow up whenever that happened. I'd say: "How do you think I was able to pay my check? You're in business, aren't you? How do you think the Celtics are able to pay me? By giving out free tickets? You want to go to a Celtics game, you ask: 'Is there any way I can *buy* a couple of tickets?' Don't ask if there are any free ones. The answer's no."

Then I'd get up, walk out, and I'd never go back to those places.

That's why I never let people buy my meals. Plenty of owners have offered, but I always tell them: "No thanks. If I can't pay, I won't eat here."

Oh sure, if a guy sends over an after-dinner drink, courtesy of the house, that's a different story. That's part of his business. I just don't want him picking up my tabs, because once you allow that to happen you've now got an obligation to him. You may not even know him all that well, yet you're obligated to him. I didn't want to be obligated to anyone but the Celtics, so I made it a point to always pay my own way, and I encouraged our players to do the same.

Larry Bird's smart this way. He'll go out with a group of guys and sometimes he'll buy the beer, sometimes they'll buy the beer. He doesn't want anything from them, and he's hoping they don't want anything from him. As soon as he gets the feeling they're with him just because he's Larry Bird, that's it; he dumps them. That's what all the smart ones do.

The celebrity life just isn't all it's cracked up to be, especially for some kid who, for the first time in his life, has money in his pockets and time on his hands. That can be a dangerous combination.

The naive ones see a movie like *North Dallas Forty* and they think that's how it's going to be. They can't wait to get to these big parties on these big estates with all the broads and the drugs and and the booze. They think that's the accepted thing—and it isn't. They think once you become a pro, hey, you've got to run with the women and be cool. But the smart ones know better.

In every town you go to, there's some guy saying, "Let's get something to eat! Let's have a party!" Next thing you know, that's exactly what you're doing, in *every* town, and before you know it, you're abusing yourself, abusing your body, abusing your career. You start out drinking and wind up using drugs. That's how it works.

Time—free time—is a big problem for the young kid just coming into the pros. It's a problem for a lot of guys who should be old enough to know better. It's not good time because it's sporadic time. You practice a couple of hours, you play a couple of hours and you travel a lot. That leaves a lot of empty time to fill. Unfortunately, it's not enough time to get involved in something really constructive—yet it's plenty long enough to make you look for something to ease the boredom. It's just enough, actually, to lead a guy into some pretty bad habits. You've got money. And you've got time. And you're not quite sure what to do with either one of them.

Meanwhile, everyone you meet is making a big fuss over you, telling you how wonderful you are, boosting your ego, leading you into believing you really *are* someone special, when deep in your heart you know better. You know you don't rate that kind of fawning, that adoration. Nobody rates it, certainly nobody in sports. Maybe if you've had it all of your life, if you were born into royalty or something like that, you'd know how to react to it. But if you've come up off the streets, like I did, like so many people in sports have, then who's kidding whom?

Put it this way: It's never been my cup of tea.

Some people like limousines. I'd rather ride in a cab. Or, a lot of times in Boston, I'll even take the subway. It's quicker.

I never could bring myself to say: *"Hey, I'm Red Auerbach! Look at all I've done. Have my limo downstairs; I'm off to the airport!"* You know, snap my fingers, get what I want. No way. Yet there are guys in sports who do that all the time—and they haven't won a damn thing yet! They figure, the money's there; why not use it?

I try very hard to live in a style that has nothing to do with how much money I might have. My idea of a good restaurant has nothing to do with a gourmet meal. I dislike them intensely. I can go into a plain little Chinese restaurant, or a deli, and be perfectly content. Extremely so.

You can take me to the fanciest joint in Boston, or New York, with all the gourmet crap and big-name wines—but that's not me. I'd rather have a good pastrami. Yet people don't understand that. They think you've arrived at a certain station in life and that you're going to act accordingly: "What? You're eating *here*? I can't believe it!" But what's a fine place to eat? To me, a fine place to eat is a place where I like the food. I don't like going to these ritzy places where they put these five little things around your plate, decorating the dish with things I've never tasted in my life. Like this one place I went to with an owner and friends. They took a steak and covered it with pâté, and then put a crust on top of it. It probably cost $50 to $60. The owner's wife thought it was terrific, but I called the waiter over and said, "What the hell is *this*? Do you suppose I could get a little piece of fish, with nothing on it?" You should have seen him. He acted highly insulted, like he was wondering what the hell someone like me was doing in a place like that?

But, see, people think that's the thing you've got to do when you have money. You're *supposed* to enjoy stuff like that. Why? Because they charge you $85 for your dinner—so it *must* be fabulous, right?

Personally, I'd rather keep my feet on the ground. No matter how many awards you've received in your life or how much success you've known, material or otherwise, you always want to go back to where you were, to *who* you were before the world decided you were a big shot.

My father used to have his own dry cleaning business. It was called Sunset Cleaners. When I was going to college, I'd come home on vacations and holidays and help him—not because I needed the money, but because he needed the help. I'm playing ball at George Washington University, dating the coeds, a big man, right? But in Brooklyn, back home, I'm nobody. I'm just my father's kid. So I'd show up at 10 o'clock at night with two sandwiches and a big bottle of cream soda, and there'd be, oh, say 100 suits all piled up, and the customers wanted those clothes for the holidays; if they didn't get them on time, they'd take their business somewhere else. So I'd work by myself all night long, on my feet until 8 in the morning, and when my father showed up they'd be all done. We got 15 cents a suit back then, so that was $15 I'd made for him.

I've got a tailor I go to now—Jerry the Tailor, on Boylston Street in Boston—and he's got a machine in his shop that's just like the one I used to use when I worked in my father's shop. It's called a pan-tex. Every so often, like on a Saturday morning before going to a practice, I'll stop in Jerry's place and press some of my own stuff and then pay him. He's a good kid. He doesn't want to take the money; he doesn't even want me to have to do any work. But I tell him that it really makes me feel good to do something like that. It's like going back in time, you know? Plus, it's nice to know I can still use my hands if I have to.

You never want to get too far away from your basic values, but fame can separate you from them in a hurry if you're not careful, or if you start believing everything you read and hear.

Sometimes the public demands too much from people who earn their living in the limelight. That's when you've got to ask yourself: *What are your fans really owed?*

Bill Russell became very adamant on this point. He insisted: "All a performer owes is a good performance." Beyond that, he felt *nothing* was owed, including autographs, appearances and small talk on the street.

I don't entirely agree with that, yet I can certainly understand what causes many celebrities to feel that way, to retreat into a very private personal life where any intrusions are resented.

When you're in the public eye a lot of people regard you as little more than a piece of meat. They presume they can say what they want to you, do what they want to you, and ask what they want from you, and that you have to stand there and oblige their every wish because that's what you get paid to do.

Well, that's *not* what you get paid to do. Not at all. I've heard people say: "Someday when no one asks for your autograph, you'll look back and miss all that attention."

Oh yeah? Bull. Sure, it's exciting and flattering when you're first starting out and you're not used to it, but after a while you get to be like the guy who works in the chocolate factory. For the first few days he loves the stuff; he can't get enough of it, in fact. But then after he's been there a while it doesn't mean that much to him anymore, and by the time he retires he couldn't care less if he never saw a piece of it again.

That's how it is for a lot of people who live in the fishbowl: They can't wait to climb out.

Personally, I do sign autographs, because it eliminates talk. Russell won't sign them. Jack Benny never did. Dave Cowens, on the other hand, felt autographs were a copout, that people who were too self-conscious or insecure to strike up a conversation found it easier and safer to thrust a piece of paper at someone. He used to make a game of it, ignoring the paper and reaching out to shake their hand and ask them what their name was. His idea was that a brief personal interaction meant much more than a scrap of paper which would most likely wind up being tossed out with the rubbish.

Dave was at an airport one day when a young kid, maybe 10 or 12, walked up and asked for an autograph. "I'll tell you what," he said. "I'll give you a choice. I'll sign my name if you want me to. Or, if you'd rather, we can go over there and have a hot dog and a Coke before my flight takes off."

Naturally, the kid goes for the hot dog and Coke, but while they're standing there talking about it, the kid's mother—not knowing what's going on—comes charging onto the scene and starts giving Dave holy hell: "You big shots have a lot of nerve saying no to autographs. Who do you think pays your salary . . .?"

Dave didn't say a word. He just turned and walked away, leaving the kid to tell the mother what had really happened.

There's no escaping public attention sometimes. One afternoon I went to one of these stand-up luncheonettes in New York with Walter Kennedy, my late friend and league commissioner, for a quick bite to eat. He went to get the beer and I went to get the sandwiches. It's a long wait. The place is mobbed. Finally we meet and I'm just about to take my first bite—and you guessed it: "Hey, Red, would you mind signing this card for my kid?" Walter, who was a kind guy, just looked the other way as I said: "I certainly *would* mind! Where were you when I was standing in line? You were eating, and now that you're through it makes no difference to you that my friend and I are anxious to eat. If you want to wait, I'll sign it when we're finished. Otherwise, forget it."

It happens all the time.

Russell was even more curt than I was whenever someone pulled a stunt like that on him. He'd be eating, enjoying the company of his friends, and someone would walk right up to his table.

"Hey, Bill. I hate to bother you . . ."

"Then *don't!*"

That would always end the conversation, especially when Russell followed it up with what we liked to call *"the look."*

People usually got the message in a hurry.

For years guys who grew up in the same neighborhood I did, old friends of mine, would never come up to me in Madison Square Garden because they were afraid that I'd become such a big wheel I would snub them. I'd meet them on the streets, and when they'd tell me that I'd say, "C'mon, you've gotta be kidding me! We grew up together!" It was unbelievable.

Some years back, about eight or nine I guess, they had a little banquet in New York for the Public School Athletic League Hall of Fame. I showed up, Sonny Werblin was there, Marty Glickman, lots of guys like that: Old New York City athletes. Some of my neighborhood gang showed up, too, and I finally got a chance to express these feelings I had to all of them. Now we're back into those friendships again; I see some of them quite a bit. They're happy and I'm happy. But they just didn't know how I'd react until they saw for themselves that I was still me, the kid they used to know. Things in my life had changed, but I hadn't changed at all.

For some reason people don't want to believe that, no matter how much you try to tell them it's true.

Then again, I was with Bird once when he went to shoot a camera commercial. This guy came up to him and said, "You don't remember me, do you? I went to the same school you did—*after* you got out."

Poor Larry. He felt bad admitting he didn't know who the guy was, but how the hell was he supposed to know someone like that?

Sometimes you can't win. So you just do the best you can to live a normal life, even though you're living inside a plastic bubble where everything you do is open to scrutiny and everyone you meet treats you with a deference that can make you feel very uncomfortable.

Personally, I can become embarrassed over a big fuss. I've had construction guys come up to me on the street and say, "Can I shake your hand?" That's different. That I love, because these are regular guys, who look at you as if you're a regular guy, and they're not looking to get anything from it.

I remember one time Dot and I were walking out of the Mayflower Hotel in Washington, D.C. and this lady—had to be in her late 70s—walked up and said: "Mr. Auerbach, may I shake your hand? Your teams have given me so much pleasure over the years . . ."

Something like that makes you feel humble. It really does.

The ones I steer away from are the ones who come rushing up to you at a party or a banquet, trying to show everybody that they know you.

You don't always want to be the center of attention. You can't be talking all the time, taking over rooms, things like that. When I go to cocktail parties or receptions, which I avoid as much as possible, I'll stand around talking with one or two people. But mostly I'll listen to what's being said and watch the people around me. I don't like to have people flocking around me, waiting for me to regale them with stories or volunteer inside dope. I try to let others instigate the conversation until enough time has passed for me to duck out graciously.

It's easy to say: Keep your feet on the ground. But it's not that easy to do. But you can do it if you work at it. Bobby Orr worked at it when he *owned* Boston, and I always admired him for that. John Havlicek worked at it. Larry Bird works at it. I'm talking about humility, humbleness.

That includes being accessible, within reason. People seem to be amazed when I answer my letters. Why? Why shouldn't I answer them? Every single letter that comes across my desk—with the exception of form letters—gets answered by me. This was another little lesson I learned from Walter Brown, who owned the Celtics and brought me to Boston in 1950: The bigger a person becomes, the more accessible he becomes. It's the self-styled big shot who becomes difficult to see. All of a sudden, it's beneath his dignity to answer letters. But Walter answered every letter he received and so do I. If a Celtics customer has a problem, he knows he can write to me and I'll get the damn thing solved. I used to tell this to my daughters all the time: If you've got a problem with your car, write to the president of General Motors. If he's any kind of an administrator, you'll get an answer. Write to some flunky junior executive and the letter will wind up in a wastebasket. That's why he'll always be a *junior* executive.

I also answer 99 percent of my phone calls, unless I know the call's from a solicitor or someone who's going to take up a lot of my time.

There are exceptions to my pleasantness, however. A guy calls up and tells Mary, my secretary, "I'm a friend of Red's." So she puts him through. Now I get on the line, and all he's doing is making a pitch for me to buy stocks or something. That makes me mad as hell. He's no friend of mine. And if there's one thing I hate, it's a con man. So I tell him that and hang up.

But going back to what I said earlier, it can be a lonely life for a kid who's thrust into that celebrity atmosphere, particularly if he's determined not to let the money and the fame affect him. That's easier said than done when you're a 22-year-old millionaire. You can have so many "friends" hanging around that you end up supporting an entourage as big as the one that used to follow Sugar Ray Robinson everywhere he went.

Or Muhammad Ali. Hangers-on by the dozens. You don't have to worry about finding them. They find you.

You learn through experience—even if you were brought up on a farm—how to spot them and how to fend them off. And that's what you've got to do if you have any hope of maintaining control of your own life.

Unfortunately, some people get to *like* the idea of being a celebrity, and they can't distinguish what's real from what's obviously artificial. That happens all the time in a place like Hollywood. Ever go to a restaurant out there? You see these little broken-down guys with white hair and big potbellies walking around with gorgeous chicks on their arm—and they think it's *love!* Hey, if they were Joe Blow without a dime in their pockets . . . ah, what's the point? That's life. That's the way some people are.

I get a kick out of watching "celebrities" come into town, especially some of these guys they've got on the soaps; you know, *One Life to Live*, *General Hospital*, shows like that. They all look alike to me—young, handsome, virile guys—and nobody would pay any attention to them if they were walking down the street by themselves. Nobody would know who they were. And that's not good. They've *got* to make a splash, right? So they get some press agent to run around the city, telling everyone, "So-and-so of *General Hospital* will be at such-and-such a place tomorrow at 2 o'clock . . ."

Now the crowd assembles and he shows up, waving his arms like he can't believe what he's seeing, yet making damn sure no one misses his arrival, and he says, "Oh, wow, *my* public! I love you all."

Bull.

Your true celebrities—the great athletes, the Bob Hopes, people like that—hey, they're *real* excitement. There's nothing phony about them. They're celebrities in name, celebrities in face, celebrities in style. Especially style.

There's a tendency, once you become a so-called success or a so-called celebrity, to become a little bit of a faker, too. You have two personalities now: One for when you're with the public and another for when you're at home or with friends.

Sometimes you can't avoid that, like when you're out making a speech. But I'm talking about day-to-day living, day-to-day dealings with people. I try to avoid it as much as I can. I try to be the way I am, wherever I am, all the time.

I became very angry with Chuck Connors one time. Chuck played college ball at Seton Hall, then spent two seasons playing for the Celtics when the league was just getting off the ground. He was 6-7 and a good athlete, but he was smart enough to realize his brightest future was going to be in movies and TV, and of course he went on to have great success as an actor. We became good friends. I love the guy; I really do. And he was coming to Boston to shoot a commercial this one time, so he called me up and asked me to join him for dinner later that night after our game. So we met and went over to Jimmy's, a famous restaurant on the Boston waterfront.

This was when his TV series, *The Rifleman*, was really big. Well, sure enough, someone recognized him, wearing his cowboy hat and all. He could have simply said, "Thank you." Instead, he made this big Hollywood production out of signing an autograph, turning it into a tremendous scene.

I was embarrassed by it all, and I told him so when we got to our table. "Chuck," I said, "I go out to dinner to be calm and quiet. I don't go out to embrace the public so that everyone will know that I'm here and some joker will write in his column that I was at Jimmy's with Chuck Connors. That's not my bag. I'm with the public all the time, just like you are. But when I'm out like this, trying to enjoy a meal and some friendly conversation, all I'm looking for is a peaceful evening. Don't you ever want some peaceful time for yourself, too?"

I chewed him out, and we talked about it for quite a while.

But this is what I mean when I say the celebrity life can be a lonely life, especially for someone who values his privacy. You're always on stage, it seems, and the people who want to shake your hand to get an autograph are only part of the problem. There are a lot of other people out there just waiting to see you fall, to see you make a mistake, or maybe even to see you make a fool of yourself. If you're having a drink in a bar or at a cocktail party, there's always someone waiting to see you make an ass of yourself. Don't ask me why; that's just the way some people think.

I once read a fascinating interview with Reggie Jackson in which he talked about the way people relate money to performance, and how they almost turn your salary into a basis for character judgment. He said: "Money doesn't give you base hits. Money doesn't change your abilities. It will allow you to live better, but it won't change your talents. That's what a lot of people don't understand about players. They refuse to understand. They say, 'Well, this guy's making this, and that guy's making that, so they ought to get their butts onto the field, and they shouldn't be hurt, and they shouldn't have a bitch or a complaint . . .'"

He's absolutely right. That *is* how people think.

He also said, in that same interview, that black guys sometimes face even more pressures than white guys once they attain that celebrity status: "My own race has sometimes given me hell over where I buy my home, where I get my hair cut, things like that. If the girl I'm dating is light-complexioned, or the friends I'm with are white, or if my business associate happens to be white—I get heat all the time from people who say, 'You don't know what it's like to be black!' Hell, what are they talking about? It's taken me 30 years to become wealthy. I know where I came from. I know who I am. I'm just going somewhere else. But I'll always be a black man first, an athlete second."

See what I mean when I say there's a price to be paid, and that it can be lonely up there at the top?

Back when I coached and traveled with the club, I'd get a quick sandwich or some Chinese food after I left an arena, then I'd go back to my room and stay there. Bob Cousy couldn't understand why I wouldn't go out with him after games. I'd tell him, "Cooz, you'll see when you get older. You become tired of the people and tired of the pace."

Years later, when he began to coach, we used to laugh about it. "Arnold," he'd say, "I understand it now. I'm doing the same things you used to do."

And he did.

The celebrity life. It's just not all it's cracked up to be.

9.

Drugs and Pussyfooters

"We've got to get rid of the problem."

When you talk about the "loneliness" of stardom, along with the inherent problems that come with being young and unrestricted with too much time and money on your hands, you're inevitably talking about the ever-present danger of drugs coming into the picture.

In the old days the big worry was alcohol—and that's still a matter of great concern to me. I'll have a social drink now and then, just like anyone else, but if I'm going out on a speaking date or to any other public appearance, I'll never have a drink of any kind, because I don't want anyone saying, "Hey, that's the whiskey talking."

And I'd *never* have a beer or drink on the day of a game when I was coaching. Never. In fact, I won't have one on the day of a game now for the same reason. I never want to walk into that locker room and have the players thinking to themselves, "Jeez, Red's been drinking."

I never wanted any ballplayers who need false courage, and I didn't want any of my guys thinking I needed false courage to say whatever was on my mind. I felt that was very important.

And I didn't believe in being sneaky, like having a drink and then reaching for mouthwash, or drinking only vodka because it doesn't have an odor. That's bush. I wasn't much of a drinker to begin with, but, to the extent that I did drink, I wasn't going to be a phony about it.

Many times, after I quit coaching, someone would say: "Hey, the game doesn't start till 7:30; let's grab an early dinner." Or even in my office, where I still entertain friends before our home games, there's liquor to be had. But I won't touch it when our team's playing. Superstition? Maybe. But there's also a very good foundation to that idea.

When you're discussing alcohol, it's an altogether different problem than the one we face today with drugs. Where do you draw the line in determining if a man's an alcoholic? Two guys go to a cocktail party. One may have four drinks and they won't appear to have affected him at all. But his friend, who has a lower tolerance, may be stinko after one. Yet he's trying to be a social guy, so he ends up getting drunk very quickly.

I don't know the answers and I'm not passing judgment. I just know alcohol can be a problem, particularly for the people around you, if it isn't handled correctly and intelligently. But drugs are something else, and I have very definite ideas here.

Why do kids with great futures get mixed up with that stuff? I'm talking particularly about athletes, guys who supposedly understand the importance of taking good care of their bodies, guys who have the potential of earning a comfortable living with their physical skills.

What makes a David Thompson, a Chuck Muncie, a Willie Wilson—outstanding athletes with brilliant futures in their games—hurt themselves the way those guys did? That's like asking, what makes a Hollywood star get hooked on heroin or cocaine? Why did a John Belushi have to die?

The simple answer is "kicks": Everyone's looking for a new kick. There are more cocaine parties among the affluent than there are among the poor guys on the street, because the affluent crowd can afford it and is looking for something to do. I'm talking about people who have fortunes in the bank and don't know what to do with them. The money just sits there. They blow a couple thousand here and a couple thousand there, and pretty soon that novelty wears off.

Plus—and here's something the average fan never stops to think about—when you gain big, big fame, you now have other problems, too. Show me the man who has everything, and I guarantee you he'll find something to be unhappy about. Or nervous about. He'll be going out with beautiful women and suddenly it will hit him: *"They're going out with me only because I have money. If I were on the streets, I wouldn't have a chance with any of these dames."*

See, there are always anxieties, neuroses, problems. The amount of money you have doesn't make any difference at all. You just encounter these worries on a different level, that's all.

Of course, the drug thing starts a lot earlier than the pros. You're in college, and there's always some hail-fellow-well-met, a "good guy" who's always after you: "Let's go to a party!" He's got all the contacts for women and beer, and he's always picking up the tab. It starts with beer, but the next thing you know, everyone at the party's smoking pot. And it just progresses from there. Same thing on the high school level. There's always that one "great guy," fronting the whole thing, telling you on the sly: "Hey, I've got some *great* stuff over here."

Now when the athlete gets hooked and his finances start dwindling, they tell him: "Want to get your stuff? No problem. But first you've got to help me get more guys . . ."

All of a sudden the athlete becomes the hail-fellow-well-met, and this is how the thing spreads.

The athletes, you see, are very vulnerable. That's why your superstars have got to be very careful about who they associate with, where they're seen and where they go. These drug people aren't stupid. They know that if they can addict a superstar, in any sport, they can go around saying, "Hey, so-and-so was at a party the other night and, boy, you should have seen him!" The idea is, if they can link themselves to his name, to his fame, then they can get other people to fall into line a little bit easier.

It figures. Why do you see so many big stars doing commercials? Because the sponsors know these people have great public acceptance, that the public *wants* to believe in what these people say and what they presumably stand for.

That is what makes sports stars such attractive targets. The more that people bother them, the more they retreat into privacy, and this is where they often get into big trouble—making the wrong associations while trying to avoid that life in a fishbowl.

Kicks. Time. Money. Fame. They can make a young kid a sitting duck for some of the sharks who are swimming out there.

We've been lucky in Boston. We haven't had any big problems with drugs. I don't know what my reaction would be if a kid who'd been with me for a while, a good kid, eventually strayed off the path. I know I'd do everything that I could, and that the organization could, to help him straighten out. If he was a new kid? I'd get rid of him as quickly as I could. I'd be giving somebody else my problems, sure; but that's life.

The league thinks it's taking the right approach to the drug problem. I don't. But at least we're cognizant of it and we're trying to do something about it. I just don't think we're doing enough.

In my mind, we've got to get rid of the problem. Period. And I think that should go for all sports, first because you're talking about the impact these guys have upon kids, and secondly because you're talking about an addiction that requires great amounts of money, which may lead into serious misbehavior involving betting on games and crap like that. There's no doubt in my mind that all of this stuff is tied together.

The way our rules are set up now, a guy with a problem can turn himself in for treatment and he'll continue to receive his salary while the league provides him with counseling and medical assistance. If he turns himself in a second time, he'll receive the same treatment, only now he'll be suspended without pay.

If a player doesn't come forward on his own, but his team has reason to believe he's got a drug problem, that information is passed on to an independent drug expert who then, if he concurs that there are reasonable grounds to suspect a problem, can authorize a urinalysis of that player. If the player refuses, he's banned for life. If he takes the test and fails it, he's also banned for life—though these "lifetime bans" are subject to appeal after two years.

Well, that's certainly a step in the right direction, but it's not enough to meet the problem head-on. Not in my mind, anyway. If a guy is willing to come forward and admit he's got a problem, great. I'd respect him for that. And I'd be all in favor of anything the league could do to help him beat the habit.

Beyond that, my recommendation would be to conduct unannounced urinalyses on *everybody!* Just like they did in those 1983 Pan-Am Games in Caracas. Remember? They told everyone, "If you want to compete in the Games, you've got to take the tests." Simple as that.

A lot of guys went home, if you'll recall, afraid to take the tests, knowing that if they flunked them they'd probably forfeit their Olympic eligibility.

Let's face it, you either want to eliminate the problem or you don't. So what's all this pussyfooting? This is the only way to tackle drugs.

According to John Drew, who admitted his addiction, the only thing a drug addict, or a man engaging in drugs, respects is fear—fear of running out, fear that they won't have enough money to purchase what they need. I don't know; I've never been in that position. But it makes sense to me. So it also makes sense to me that the way to send a message to these guys is through shock and fear, placing them on notice that you're about to cut off their primary source of income if you discover, through these unannounced tests, that they're not clean. That, it seems to me, would prompt a lot of them to come forward on their own. Those are the ones we'd help, just like we're doing now.

As for those who got caught without coming forward? Too bad. Goodbye. I'd hit them with that "lifetime suspension," allowing them to apply for reinstatement in two years, assuming they'd smartened up.

The problem here, of course, is that the Players Association would scream: *"Invasion of privacy!"*

Bull. Why should the association object to this if it's really interested in eradicating the problem rather than just attacking it with window dressing? Why would a guy who's *not* on drugs object to submitting to a simple test two or three times a month? What better way would there be for players, as a group, as an association, to make a strong, no-nonsense statement: *We don't want this stuff in our game!*

But no, they yell about invasions of their privacy. Why? What are they afraid of? I know what the junkies are afraid of. They don't want to be caught. They don't want to be exposed, or to have their main source of income taken away. But what are the guys who are clean afraid of? Are they afraid they *might* want to try it some day? Or is it peer pressure they're afraid of?

It's very simple in my book. If the players want to clean up their game, then they've got to adopt a hard line. It's the only way to lick the problem. And if one guy on a team refuses to go along with it, then everybody's got to look at that guy and ask him why. All of a sudden he's a big civil rights advocate? Come on. He's got a reason for fearing those tests, and you can be damn sure it's *not* his enthusiasm for constitutional principles.

Would it actually be an invasion of privacy? I don't know. No one's ruled that it would be. The law, to the best of my knowledge, hasn't said a thing about it. So let's find out. Let's test it if we have to. I know that back home in Washington they randomly stop these big trucks on the beltway and give them a complete going-over. If something's wrong with them, boom, they stay there.

Nobody can drive them away. They've got to be towed away.

Would my idea be any different? I don't see why.

But even if it was determined to be illegal, we could get around that if the Players Association would voluntarily waive that invasion of privacy bit. We're giving these guys millions of dollars in salaries. Is it too much to expect that they'll keep themselves clean? Is it too much to expect that they'll take an active interest in the image of our game?

I've long maintained that the Players Association is interested in only one thing, and that's the furtherance of its own objectives. They can try to censor me any way they want on this thing, but it won't eliminate the obvious fact that they're dragging their feet. My suspicion has always been that the association doesn't care about the league or its solvency or anything like that. All it cares about is how much it can keep getting. So when it claims to be cooperating with us on something like this drug problem, I'm sorry, but I don't buy it.

What we need is the *100 percent* cooperation of the association, because without it we'd all end up spending too much time in court. Arbitration. Everything's arbitration. A ballplayer punches a coach, so you suspend him and fine him $2,000: *Arbitration!* It becomes so time-consuming and expensive that after a while some teams simply say, "To hell with it."

But the answer here is obvious. Forget the ego of ownership; forget the pressure of winning; forget the temporary setback that might come from the loss of certain stars, as difficult as that would be; forget all of that, and take the hard line!

Let's make unannounced spot checks a contractual stipulation for everyone who wants to play in the NBA. That, it seems to me, would be a reasonable condition to impose, in exchange for the fabulous amounts of money we're paying these people.

If that's built into a standard contract which all parties agree to up front—the owners *and* the Players

Association—we'll have no worries about "invasion of privacy," and we'll be well on the road to eliminating the biggest menace in sports today.

Otherwise, we're just kidding ourselves.

10.

Motivating Thoughts

"Is this the year we stop paying the price?"

I had a theory back when I was starting out, and what it came down to was this: *Basketball is like a war.*

When you go into a war, you go in to win it, because you don't know what's going to happen to you if you lose. You could become a slave. Or a POW. You might even get killed.

It's the same when you're a coach in sports. What happens to you if you lose? As far as your career goes, you're dead.

So I'd spend hours asking myself: What will it take for us to win? They're coming at me with all of their offensive weapons, shooting from every direction. What will it take to stop them? How are we going to win this war?

One answer, I decided, was defense. You see, defense is just hard work. There'll be nights when the ball won't fall in, no matter how well you execute your plays. Your touch will be off just a bit and there won't be anything you can do about that. It happens. It's something you can't always control. But you *can* play good defense if you put your mind to it; that's something you can do *every* night.

So I made up my mind early that any team of mine was going to be a team that played tough defense. That was one way to win the war. But even that would be dependent upon another factor: Motivation.

Motivation! Getting your people to give you their best efforts. Night in and night out. Game in and game out. Motivation, that was the key. Looking for reasons to win. You have to do that when you play as many games as pro teams do, particularly if you've got a good team and you're playing against a weaker opponent. Sounds like that should be a cinch, right? Far from it.

I've told this to many college coaches. You have to motivate your players for the so-called *easy* games. The big games take care of themselves; they're self-motivating to a large extent. It's the game which catches you off-balance in which you've got to bust your humps.

Check the records. UCLA, Indiana, Kentucky, North Carolina, Maryland—all those great schools: Somewhere during their schedules you'll find stretches where they go two or three games winning by only one or two points, and if their final record is something like 21–2 or 24–3, invariably one of those losses will be to a team that never should have beaten them. *Don't get overconfident!* You tell them that every night, and yet it happens. And they end up paying a price for it.

So you have to treat every game as a separate entity, and then come up with a logical reason why we *must* win *this* one tonight. If there was a secret to the success I enjoyed as a coach, that might have been it right there. I'll bet I came up with 2,000 reasons why we *had* to win.

But then sometimes outside factors did the job for me. Like the night in Cincinnati when the management there handed out 5,000 cigars to customers as they filed to their seats. It was a key game, and the Royals were one of our big rivals at the time, so the idea was to have everyone light up and blow smoke in our faces after we'd gone down to defeat. It was a takeoff on my cigar bit, you know? And I'll admit, it was a pretty cute idea, but it backfired on them. Talk about motivating speeches! I might have given the best one of my life that night. There was no damn way we were going to lose that one. I had the team so hopped up we went out and kicked the hell out of them.

Some nights, though, I'd just try to appeal to everyone's common sense: "Look, you guys are already chalking up this one as a win, right? But, remember, no one's ever won a damn thing on paper. You still have to go out and get the job done. Now there are two ways you can go about this. If you really bust your balls at the start, we might win this thing by the third period and then you can sort of take it easy and have some fun going down the stretch. If you don't do that, you're going to end up having to play 48 hard minutes and try to eke it out at the buzzer. I don't have to tell you, a win over these guys counts just as much as a win over L.A., but you can make it an easy win or you can sweat your fannies off. It's your choice."

See, part of motivation is putting ideas into people's heads, getting them to see things a certain positive way. There was the night, for example, when we were getting ready to play Philadelphia in one of those Game 7 showdowns at the Garden. The minute I walked into our dressing room I could sense something was wrong. It was too quiet. Everyone was too serious. We had been champions for a long, long time, but now everyone was starting to wonder: *Is this the year it ends? Is it finally someone else's turn?*

I stood there for a moment, looking around, trying to spot some life, some enthusiasm, some reaction. Nothing. Just silence. So what did I do? I started to laugh, right out loud. Everyone looked at me like I was nuts—but now I had their attention.

"You guys have to be kidding me," I said. "If you're worried about playing *them,* how do you think they must feel having to play *us?*" Then I walked out.

Satch Sanders later told me everyone began looking at one another, and they all started laughing, too. By the time the knock on the door came, they were having a party. Then they went out and kicked Philadelphia's ass.

You have to be careful. You can motivate *too* much. It's a hard thing to gauge. There are inner forces you can appeal to, giving a guy something to think about, and there are outer forces. But what you don't want is a guy who becomes too hyped up. After all, we're talking about a game of touch here. It's like a tennis player. He can get sky-high. That means he's mentally in shape and has a strong desire to win, but it doesn't mean the ball's going to land where he wants it to. If he gets himself psyched up too much, he'll be hitting the balls all over the place.

You can outsmart yourself, too. I did that once in Detroit and some of our old guys still kid me about it. It was New Year's Eve. We'd won 17 in a row, tying the league record my Caps set back in 1946–47. The next day we were facing Cincinnati, one of the worst teams in the league at that time, in the first game of a doubleheader. If we won, we'd make history. So instead of letting the guys go out to a movie or do whatever they'd normally do, I had them all come up to my room. No celebrating whatsoever. I ordered sandwiches and Cokes and we played cards for a while, then we just stood around looking at each other until I sent them all to bed.

The next day Cincinnati blew us off the court. It wasn't even close.

Motivation becomes a tricky thing when a coach has the same cast of characters to deal with year after year. For one thing, players get tired of hearing the same old voice over and over again. That's a problem. The smart coach is always looking for new approaches.

We won world championships in each of my last eight years on the bench. That meant two things. First, there was always the obvious threat of overconfidence. So I had a standard speech I gave on the opening day of training camp that went like this: "Gentlemen, you are the world champions. You've gone around all summer with your chests sticking out. You've heard all of the accolades. You've had a hell of a time. But now, unfortunately, everyone's going to be out to knock your jocks off. They're all going to be out to get you. Now if you want to let them get you, just try living off last year's reputation. I'm not asking you guys, 'What have you done for me lately?' It's not my club. It's *your* club. *You* are the champions. You have to decide how much that means to you and how much you're willing to pay to go on being the champions. Because if that's what you want to do, if you want to keep this title and the good feeling that goes with it, you're going to have to go out there and meet all these challengers head-on and tell them: *'You're damn right we're the champions, and if you want this title you're going to have to take it away from us!'* "

That was my opening salute, so to speak. Then I'd run their asses off, reminding them all the while: "Is *this* the year we get lazy? Is *this* the year we get soft? Is *this the year we stop paying the price. . . ?*"

Okay, I'd ride them for a while, just to get them back into a proper frame of mind. But then I'd cool it a bit.

If I've got basically the same team back, then it only makes sense that now my practices should become *shorter*. Too many coaches have the idea that you *must* have a two-hour practice every morning, followed by a two-hour practice every afternoon, followed by a full team meeting every night all through training camp, and then you *must* have a two-hour practice every off-day in the season.

Says who? If you've got the same team coming back, it's reasonable to assume that everyone already knows the plays. Oh, sure, you might put in a new one every now and then, or add a special wrinkle for a certain tough opponent, but that doesn't require all of these hours day after day.

So what's the point? Why is every practice lasting two hours? So the coach can hear his own voice? So he can satisfy his own ego?

I used to tell my guys: "Look, work hard and we'll get out of here in a hurry."

I didn't have to tell them: "Here's what we do when we call the '2' play . . ." They already knew that. What was the point of repeating it over and over?

If I could run a good practice in, say, an hour and a half, then the following year I should be able to run the same practice in maybe an hour and 10 minutes. Doesn't that make sense?

But so many of these coaches don't look at it that way. They'll figure out some way to stretch that time into two hours, as if *two hours* was written someplace in stone.

It's a game of fun, remember? It's a game of touch. They go together.

One way you can motivate a guy is by reminding him you have the power to ship him to a lousy organization, a place where he'll be treated as a chattel rather than being treated with respect, a place where there's no pride or feeling of belonging.

Sometimes, in a kidding sense—yet intending to make a point—I'd walk by someone like Jim Loscutoff and whisper: "Keep it up, Loscy, and you'll be playing in Minneapolis. It gets pretty cold there, I'm told."

But let's say you're the coach of a crappy organization—maybe that was the only job you could find—and most of your players have long-term contracts. Now what do you do? How do you motivate in a situation like that?

I'll admit it's not easy. But there are ways.

You could always eat a guy's contract and toss him out. First, however, you want to take him aside and talk with him.

Your conversation might go like this:

"Look, if you have no pride and no feeling of accomplishment, other than the amount of money you're earning right now, you're making a serious mistake. If this is how you're going to approach it, what do you think's going to happen once the contract expires and you've blown the dough? I'll tell you what's going to happen. Your career's going to be shot. We'll never give you another contract, and if we let you go everyone else is going to know that there's something wrong with you, regardless of your abilities. The word will go out that you're a troublemaker, bad for a ballclub's chemistry.

"You don't want that. And I don't want to do it to you.

"So, look, all I'm asking from you is that you give me your best effort for 82 games. That's all. Be dedicated enough to give me whatever you have. I understand there'll be times when you'll go up for a rebound and the ball will bounce over your hands. I know there'll be nights when you'll shoot the ball and it won't drop into the hole. I realize these things happen. But I also know that if you hustle and you're motivated and you play the strong D, we'll have a shot at winning that game. Everything else will fall into place. All you have to do is give me that honest effort.

"So that's what I'm asking of you now. Give me that kind of dedication.

"If you can't, or you won't, I don't give a damn if we're the worst team in basketball; I'll eat that contract, or I'll get rid of you, providing I can find someone dumb enough to take you off my hands!"

There are times, unfortunately, when you just have to give up on a player.

We went through a tough period back in '77 and '78 with guys like Sidney Wicks and Curtis Rowe. They wouldn't have lasted a week with me. Tommy Heinsohn was coaching for us then and he did his best to reach them, but it was no use; they didn't care. So we let them go. Their attitudes were ruining the morale of the team. Wicks ended up playing a few more years with San Diego, but never amounted to anything, and Rowe never played again at all, even though he was only 29 when we dumped him. Some guys just aren't worth the trouble.

One of the first agents I ever had to deal with came into my office one day with his client. This kid wasn't even a high draft choice, yet the agent started right in telling me how this guy was going to help us win another championship. I didn't say anything. I just sat back and let him do all the talking. Then he got down to the nitty-gritty. They wanted so many extra dollars if the kid scored X number of points, and so many extra dollars if we won X number of games.

That was enough for me. "Just a minute, Buster," I said. "If *making* our ballclub isn't enough incentive for this kid, I don't want him. Now get the hell out of here."

They got up and left, and the next day they signed with another team. That was okay with me. If *that* was his attitude, he wasn't our kind of kid.

Motivation has to start with the right kind of attitude.

Winning comes first! That was the one thought which ran through all of my motivational themes.

I'd tell the guys: "There are 10 of you and only one of me, so it's a lot easier for you to look for ways to please me than it is for me to find ways to please each of you."

That's when we'd get into one of my pet peeves: Statistics.

Statistics are great for feeding a player's ego, and ego's one of the first things that can ruin good team motivation. Over and over I'd tell my guys: *"Your salary depends upon what I see with my own two eyes."* Watch a game on television or listen to a game on radio; there's no way you can tell who's conserving his energy by expending false hustle on defense in order to come out looking good in the box score. The numbers don't tell the story. A guy gets 10 rebounds. Wonderful. But how do you know whether *four* of them might have come after someone missed a free throw? See what I mean?

Yet fans and writers are forever building up players by raving about their statistics, and a player—especially a young one—hears and reads these flattering words and starts to actually believe he's someone special, maybe *more* special than other members of the team.

What happens then? Where's your motivating force? It's gone. So I was always careful when it came to handing out praise. What I *would* do, however, was go out of my way to make sure certain players' contributions were brought to the attention of the press.

The media used to upset me a lot. They still do at times, because writers are just like fans in the way they develop enthusiasm for their personal favorites, and this can be very detrimental to a team.

For many years the Boston press wrote authoritatively about a game it didn't understand. The writers began forming their own fan clubs: You'd see pro-Cousy stories, pro-Heinsohn stories, pro-Ramsey stories. Forget the game—they were too busy writing about their heroes! But they didn't know what was happening out there. They'd write: "The Boston Celtics streaked to another victory yesterday, 112–94, thanks to a sterling performance by Bob Cousy who scored 22 points . . ." They'd go on and on, and *never* mention the fact that it was Russell's *12 blocked shots* or *10 fourth period rebounds* that dominated the game.

And I resented the fact that they often gave credit to the wrong people. That can hurt a team, so I used to make a joke of it at practice the following morning: "Did you fellows see the papers today? Was that guy *really* at our game? He sure didn't see what I saw . . ."

But except for situations like those, I was frugal when it came to lavish praise. Motivationally, you lose something when players get too high an opinion of themselves. That doesn't mean I'd say a guy was a bum. What I'd say is: "He's a hell of a player—but he can still become a little bit better if he puts his mind to it."

If you tell a guy he's the greatest, how do you motivate him after that?

Once you're the greatest, there's no place to go but down.

I used to say: *"When I tell you to do something, the one word I never want to hear is, 'Why?'"* That was just a matter of discipline and respect. But when it comes to motivation, the *"why?"* is very important. It goes back to the business of communicating. Remember? *It's not what you tell them, but what they hear.*

A lot of coaches fail to understand this. They'll

spend time teaching patterns, zones, breaks and all of that, but then forget to add one vital point: Why. For everything they want to do out there that is of any great significance, they should take a couple of minutes to tell their players why they're doing it. This not only increases their respect for you, but it also increases their understanding of the game.

Why are you making a double pick? *Why* do you want to break? *Why* does your defense force a guy to the outside?

Tell them why!

If a guy's on the outside and you want to force him into the middle, it's probably because you want your defender to have some help from his teammates. Or maybe you want to force a man to the outside, because that will cause somebody else to switch. Whatever the technicality is, that's not important. What *is* important is giving your players a logical reason for everything they're doing out there.

You want smart, thinking ballplayers. Motivating can be so much easier if what you're saying appeals to their common sense and their knowledge of the game.

One of the best ways to motivate people is by not asking them to kiss your behind. Make them think you're human. Don't stand on a pedestal. Don't be a *boss!* Have patience, and show compassion, and motivate yourself to be a decent human being.

And admit mistakes. That's important.

I remember one night when I fell asleep on the bench. I was coaching Tri-Cities at the time, the year before I came to Boston, and we had taken a 150-mile bus ride to Waterloo. Well, back in those days I often suffered from motion sickness. So someone said: "Here, try a little Dramamine," or whatever it was.

I've never liked taking medication. I still don't. Maybe aspirin tablets once in a while, and I don't take many of those. This time, however, I made an exception and took the Dramamine. I'd never been on a bus ride that long before.

Well, the stuff worked all right. We'd set up a little

table in the bus for a game of Hearts and every time it was my turn to make a move, someone had to poke me. We stopped at a little hamburger joint along the way, and I got out to walk around and get some fresh air, but the minute we boarded again I fell asleep and didn't open my eyes until Waterloo.

Now we're in the dressing room and I start in: "Okay, guys, this team's good and that's a rough crowd out there . . ." That wakes me up a little bit. So we head out onto the floor.

I'm sitting there now—the game's started—and the motion of all these guys running up and down the court just about put me into a trance. I didn't make one substitution the whole first half!

Halftime can't come fast enough. I stuck my head under a faucet and slapped myself a few times, and somehow or another we got through the night. But when it was over you can bet the first thing I did was to apologize to my team. They did their job. I blew mine.

Admitting you're wrong can be motivational, too.

There were many times over the years when I'd look around the room at all of those great athletes— Cousy, Sharman, Russell, Heinsohn, Ramsey, Jones— and I'd think: *"Damn, they're ready to do their jobs. Now it's up to me to do mine."* That's how I'd psyche myself. That's how *I'd* get ready. It wasn't easy to stay motivated all the time. For the first two or three years, sure; everything's new and exciting. But after 10, 12, 15 years, that rhythmical life of 82 games can get to you— playoffs are an altogether different thing; *everyone* gets up for them—and before you know it there's a temptation to think: "Hell, we can't win every game, and I don't feel so well, so maybe tonight's is one of the ones we'll lose."

That's when you have to look for a reason to win. *Find one!* Pick a fight, take a walk, think of something that makes you angry, something or someone that makes your blood boil.

You have to do it. Because the minute the players start thinking, "Hey, the coach doesn't really care," they're going to stop caring, too.

*   *   *

Two of my favorite championships came after I stopped coaching: 1968 and 1981. In both of those years our guys found themselves trailing Philadelphia by a 1–3 margin in the conference championship round.

Hopeless situations, right? Guess again. But how do you approach a desperate plight like that?

Simple. You don't try to win three straight games. You don't even *think* of that. Game 7 is not important at that point. Neither is Game 6. And for that matter, you're not even concentrating on winning Game 5.

Here's what you tell yourself: "They haven't won a damn thing yet. They still have to beat us one more time, and that's not going to be easy."

Then you break it down like this: "Let's win the first quarter. That's all we're concerned with now, the first quarter. Then we'll just play them even in the second and we'll have the lead at the half. That'll give them something to worry about. Second half, same thing. Win the third quarter and increase our lead. Then stay with them in the fourth. If we can do that, the game's ours."

See, you don't worry about three straight games. That's too big. That's too much. That *is* scary, and you don't want frightened ballplayers. So you break it down into smaller segments that everyone can deal with comfortably.

Win *one* quarter? Of course we can! Swell. Let's do it.

It's like that great A.A. philosophy of "one day at a time." Don't tell a man he can never have a drink for the rest of his life; that's too long, too much to deal with. No one can discipline himself *forever*. But today? Yeah. I can get through today all right. Great! Then let's not worry about tomorrow right now. Let's just get through today. We'll worry about tomorrow when it comes.

That's the same way you approach being down 1–3 to Philly. You fight your way back, one step at a time, one quarter at a time, one game at a time.

It works. We've got the flags to prove it.

*   *   *

I mentioned earlier how Bobby Knight often asks people like John Havlicek and me to bring motivational messages to his kids. John gave them a great one in 1976, just before Bobby's Indiana team met Michigan in the NCAA championship game at Philadelphia.

"Fellows," Bobby said, "there's someone I want you to meet. He's a friend of mine and he's come down here from Boston to say a few words. I can't think of anyone who's been in more situations similar to ours than . . . John Havlicek."

The kids' eyes lit up as John walked in. Here's what he told them:

"You're all where you are today because of what you've done together all year long, so all you want to do right now is go out there and play the same way you have all season.

"I have never heard of anyone being accused of overhustling.

"After this game is over, you don't ever want to have to look back on any situation and tell yourself it might have been different if only you had tried a little harder.

"In the course of your lifetime you might live 70 years. These are just two hours out of those 70 years, but they're two hours you'll never get back again, so reach down deep inside and make them two of your very *best* hours!

"I'm not guaranteeing anything if you do that, because things don't always work out the way we think they're supposed to. But you'll have a much better chance of success with this approach.

"Don't ever look back and think: *'I might have had that rebound if I'd just tried harder.'* Don't walk off that court tonight with the feeling you could have given more.

"Give it all you've got."

I couldn't have said it any better than that.

John sounded exactly like what he was. A Celtic.

And Indiana won.

*   *   *

I had what you might call a standard welcoming which I gave one-on-one to young players coming into our organization. It might have varied, depending on the kid and what I thought his role would be, but essentially it came down to this:

"Have you ever seen our team play? Then you know we expect certain things from our guys. We've won championships, and we hope to win a lot more, but to *be* a champion you've got to *act* like a champion, on and off the court. You've got to have a certain feeling about yourself and about the team, and you've got to be willing to pay the price.

"We're smart enough to know when you're loafing, when you're giving us false hustle, and if we ever see that we'll get rid of you because we won't have the room or time to go into the whys and the wherefores.

"But if you have desire, and if you show the proper attitude, you'll find all kinds of help here, not only from the coaches and me, but from all of your teammates as well. Because they *want* to win, and if they can help you to improve, they'll also be helping the team to improve. That's the concept we go by here. You'll be aware of it right away.

"You'll never see a player on the Celtics bawling out a teammate. You'll never see a Celtic throwing a towel or a jacket in disgust when he's taken out of a game. That crap is selfishness and we don't buy it here. The name of our game is unity.

"If you start with us and do your job, you more than likely will finish with us. We've had more players start and finish with us than the rest of the league combined. We've helped our guys get jobs when their playing days were over. We've helped them not to squander their money. When you leave here, you're prepared to face the future.

"Now, if we're willing to take this kind of interest in you, what are you going to do? Go out there and go through the motions? Rely solely on your natural abilities, rather than going out there and working like a dog?

"Or are you going to make it your business to become a Celtic?

"That's what we want. We want you to become a Celtic."

Charlie Scott became a Celtic. A lot of people thought he never would, but I wasn't one of them. He'd been a big scorer most of his career, a one-on-one guy, and some folks wondered if he could fit into the Celtics' style of play when he came to us in 1975. He was almost 28 then.

Let me tell you a story about Charlie.

In the fifth game of our championship series with Phoenix that year—a game that went into *three* overtimes—Charlie was called out on fouls, some of which were really questionable. We won that night, but as soon as I walked into our locker room, before the press arrived, Tommy Heinsohn pulled me aside. "Will you talk to Charlie?" he said. "He's ready to explode."

And he was. They'd given the kid six fouls and a technical, and he was so upset he was shaking.

I grabbed him by both arms. "Charlie," I said, softly. "You've had a great year. You've done everything we've asked you to do, but now you're ready to blow your stack . . ."

He started to interrupt me. I squeezed his arms tighter.

"Listen. Let me tell you something. I was worse than you are now, on many occasions, but I didn't have someone to grab me and stop me like I'm doing to you. And so I did a lot of crazy things. But I'm stopping you now. I want you to show me what you're made of. I want you to grit your teeth, take a quick shower, then get the hell out of here without saying a word to anyone. Just dress and go. Quickly."

I dropped his arms. He looked at me for a minute, then went straight to the shower room, came out a minute later, jumped into his clothes and left. He never said a word.

In the next game he scored 25 points, played fabulously, and we won the championship. As soon as the final horn sounded he came running to me, tossed his arms around me and gave me a kiss. He knew what it was all about and so did I. The rest of the players knew, too, though nobody else did.

In my eyes and in the eyes of his teammates, Charlie had disciplined himself for the good of the ballclub, and now he'd just helped us win the biggest game of the year. Each one of us had total respect for what he had done. He'd come to Boston with a bad rap, but there was no doubt in anyone's mind now.

Charlie Scott had handled himself like a man. He'd become a Celtic.

Oh, I know, some people think that's a lot of bull. That's what Paul Silas thought, too, when he came to us in 1972. But the next year, in the spring of '74, we won it all. Wayne Embry, one of our old guys from the end of the Russell era, was GM of the Bucks that season. It was us against Milwaukee in the final round, and now it had all come down to a Game 7 on a Sunday afternoon out there.

Here's what Embry told a reporter after it was all over: "I felt then, and I still feel now, that we had the better ballclub. And I know our guys have just as much pride as Boston's guys do. I felt we were going to win—and yet, as I sat in my office that morning, I just couldn't relax. I kept saying to myself: *'If we were playing anybody else but the Celtics . . .'* If it had been any other team I'd have been down there taking ring sizes! But I knew the character of John Havlicek and those guys. I knew if they were down by 20 points with three minutes left, they'd *never* give up. There's a lot of the old Celtics in them. Whatever that intangible is, it must be inherent."

Later, after we'd won, I was standing in our locker room when Silas walked over and put his arm around me.

"Red," he said, "I want to tell you something. When I first got here I thought all of that stuff about tradition and so on was a lot of BS. But I know better now. It's real, all right, and I'm awfully proud to be a part of it."

It *was* real. And it's still real today.

11.

The Fires of Ambition

"Take control of the things you can control."

My son's six-four and he's only 15 years old. He's gonna be a basketball player!"

I hear it all the time from fathers who think they're going to give the world its next Larry Bird.

Hey, dreams are fine. Everyone should have a dream. Everyone should have an ambition. But you've got to be realistic, too. So my first reaction is, "Look, there are 100,000 kids out there the same size as your kid, and 99,990 will never make it to the pros. Size is nothing. It's almost irrelevant now. It's tougher to become a pro athlete today than it's ever been before because the competition is so much greater."

Of course no one wants to hear that. They still want to know: *How do you get there from here?*

You start by specializing early. To become a great athlete today, with so many specialists out there, you've got to become a specialist among specialists. That's the kind of world we're living in. Like the kicker in football, he spends his whole life learning that one skill and it becomes his niche. He can make a big living by contributing that way. Same with a pitcher in baseball.

I've seen pitchers who were terrible athletes, who couldn't do anything else. I was with one in the Navy. Put him on a basketball court and he'd be tripping over his own feet, yet out on the mound he was poetry in motion.

It's the age of specialization. If it's true that athletes are getting bigger, stronger and faster all the time, and it obviously is, then where's the line of difference? You might have 50 guys on a playground who can dunk the ball and do all that fancy crap. So what separates them? How do you stand out in that kind of company?

Your edge has to be your knowledge of the game, your knowledge of how to be productive in a team sport. You've got to know how to control that energy, to harness it, to put it to its most effective use.

A father, a coach, an adviser has got to help a young kid see the best way to utilize his natural-born talent, and this might mean convincing him not to play too many other sports. That can be a big problem right there. You take the average good athlete in a small high school. Everyone knows he's good enough to play basketball, football, baseball, all of 'em. The kid knows it, too. But he's got to be willing to give up the accolades of his peers and the compliments from his classmates. And he's got to be able to withstand pressure from the school: *"Why aren't you playing football? We need you."*

He's got to be able to withstand all of that and say, "Look, basketball is the game I love most. It's the game in which I feel I have my greatest potential. It's the game which might bring me a scholarship. It might even make me a pro. I know the odds are against me, but if I'm going to have any chance at all, it won't come from being a three-letter man. I've got to make a choice and basketball is my choice . . ."

And I'd say he has to make that choice by the time he's 13 or 14, maybe even 9 or 10 if you're talking about an individual sport like tennis or golf.

It takes a strong parent or adviser to keep a kid like that under control, especially when he's walking the hallways during, say, football season.

A good example of that was John Havlicek. John was all-state in football, basketball and baseball back in Ohio, but he went to Ohio State on a basketball scholarship. Woody Hayes tried many times to get him to come out for football, but John withstood that pressure. Then they wanted him to go out for baseball in the spring, and I think he tried that once. Basketball and baseball are a lot easier to combine than basketball and football. But then he turned thumbs down on that, too.

I ran into Woody years later and I kidded him: "Wouldn't John have been a great end?" Despite not playing at Ohio State, he was drafted by the Cleveland Browns and was the last man they cut.

"No," Woody said, "he probably would have been the best quarterback in Ohio State history. I just couldn't get him to come out."

The point is that John, coming from a small school, was sort of forced into playing all of those other sports. But at Ohio State he was better able to withstand that kind of pressure.

And that's what a kid has to do more and more today if he hopes to go far in his game.

If you're talking tennis or golf, it starts at the moment he has control of that racquet or club. If he sees that as his life's big potential, then he's got to work at it three or four hours a day with good instruction, like a Jack Nicklaus did. Oh, once in a while, especially in the old days, a kid would caddy, grow up on the greens, listening, watching and developing on the sandlot, so to speak. But those are the Horatio Alger stories and they're few and far between.

Some kids develop an early sense for their game. They're 11 and they just *know:* I want to be a baseball player! I love it.

But what happens? The old man says, "All right, but you've got to play football, too, and tennis, plus I'm going to take you camping and teach you how to fish." Well, that's fine; the kid's having a good time—but he's never going to get there in his game if he's not specializing.

I know, it's not a well-rounded situation I'm describing. I grant that. But if a kid really wants to be a pro, that's what it takes—total commitment. But I can also assure you there are thousands of kids you never read about who have taken tennis lessons from the time they were 6 years old, hoping to become professionals, hoping to make a good living from their talents, and they've never gotten beyond the level of being a top-notch club player.

Basketball has thousands of would-be professionals, too. A lot of them are very, very good. But almost all of them end up along the wayside.

It's like playing the lottery. If you're in the right place at the right time, and if you have the talent, you've got a shot. But that's all. Just a shot.

Willie Nelson has a great line in one of his songs: It refers to the *fires of ambition.*

Ambition means commitment. How much of a commitment should you make in your climb toward the top; can you make too much of a commitment?

The answer to that is yes. There's dedication, and there's overdedication, just like there's coaching, and overcoaching. You've got to be smart enough not to overdedicate, not to overcoach, because there are other things in life which have importance and must be considered.

In my case basketball was my livelihood, my whole guts, and I wanted to be good at it, just as I wanted to be good in the classroom back in the days when I was a high school teacher.

But I paid a price for that drive in that my family life suffered because of it. I didn't watch my kids grow up. I was worse than a traveling salesman in many ways. My wife Dot basically raised our daughters alone and did a fabulous job. Ask me today if that was right and I'd probably tell you no. So why did I do it? Because I didn't know any better. Oh, I knew what I was doing when I was doing it, but when you look back you can see things differently.

Our kids were good kids—they turned out great—

but I'll be the first to admit I spoiled them with material things, probably as an atonement on my part for being away so much. There were many times I felt like a heel walking out the door, heading back to Boston or back onto the road. We maintained our family home in Washington, D.C., Dot's hometown. We still do. My feeling was that if we lived in the town where I coached, two things would happen: I'd end up bringing the family's problems to practice and the team's problems into our home. Plus the phone would always be ringing with calls from writers or requests to make an appearance somewhere. The way we had it set up, the time I spent in Washington was total family time, away from all distractions. I went back every chance I got. And the time I spent in Boston belonged to the Celtics. Without that solitude and concentrated time, I'm not sure that we could have accomplished all we did.

Now, was that too great a price to have paid? In my situation, thanks to Dot, perhaps not. If you're going to try something like that you had better be a bachelor, or have a super-understanding wife.

Yet even though things all worked out well in the end, the intrusion upon family life is the one regret I have today. Did I give my kids the time they deserved? I know I didn't, and I've still got a guilt complex about it today.

It's a feeling I'm sure a lot of parents know. You can be very successful in certain phases of your life, yet always be bugged by the feeling that you weren't successful enough with your own kids because you didn't spend enough time with them.

I made a big commitment because I had this drive to be successful as the coach and general manager of the Celtics. Yet there are a lot of other people who, I'm sure, made bigger commitments than I did, bigger sacrifices, yet somehow or another the goals they were striving for were never fully realized.

That's a part of ambition, too. See, there are no guarantees. And you have to realize that luck plays a part in it, too.

You could be a Vince Lombardi, making all of the

sacrifices you want, motivating your team to the nth degree. Still, once that ball goes into the air, the difference between your being recognized as a great, great coach or just another figure on the sidelines might come down to whether the receiver catches that ball or allows it to roll off his fingertips. And if you discount that, then you're not being realistic.

I can remember a Frank Selvy jump shot rolling off the rim with two seconds to go in Game 7 of our 1962 playoff series with the Lakers. The game was tied, so it would have beaten us. Instead we won in overtime.

I can remember the night we had a one-point lead over Philadelphia in Game 7 of our 1965 playoff series. It was Philly's ball, four seconds to go. If they score, we lose. So Hal Greer tries to pass it in to Chet Walker—and John Havlicek, timing it perfectly, leaps and bats Greer's pass to Sam Jones, who dribbles out the clock. We win again.

I remember a shot Don Nelson took in 1969. That year no one expected us to win, but we pushed the Lakers to Game 7 out in the Forum, and with a little more than a minute to go Nellie took a shot that hit the back rim, bounced several feet up in the air, then dropped right through the net! It broke L.A.'s back and we won again.

Lucky? Of course we were lucky. There has to be luck involved. But luck's not enough. You have to be pretty damn good just to be in a position to play in those games, and we played in quite a few.

My point is, no matter how hard you play or how well you coach, that ball can take a crazy bounce which might mean your career. Or maybe your players are doing everything you tell them to do, but they aren't hitting; the ball's just not falling in. When that happens you've got to be realistic enough to assure yourself, "Hey, I'm doing a good job." Yet you have to understand that there may be factors affecting your career over which you have no control. All you can do is take control of the things you *can* control.

Did I want to win? Of course I did. I like to win. Why keep score if you don't want to win? Could I have been a good coach without winning? That's like asking if a man can be a good doctor even though his patients keep dying.

But as you get older you understand that winning has its place and that losing does not mean the end of the world. I mean, my whole life is not involved in a basketball game, which, when you think of it, is nothing more than a group of men running around in their underwear, tossing a round object into a hole.

Don't misunderstand, I was not a compassionate winner. Oh, you can have compassion after you win, but if you say something like that you end up sounding phony. So you're better off keeping your mouth shut and simply walking away. Anyone can try to act magnanimous; it still comes out sounding like bull. Yes, I had great empathy for some of the stars we beat—men like Jerry West, Bob Pettit, Elgin Baylor—but the respect I felt for them should have been obvious in the way we set up our defenses to stop them.

Respect for them? Yes. But not to the point that I was ever sorry we won.

A kid tells himself: "I want to be a Larry Bird."

Forget it. You can't creep into Larry's head just by watching him play. How do you measure his motivation? How do you know what he does in the off-season to further his game? Maybe he goes around squeezing tennis balls all day to strengthen his hands. Who knows? Maybe he has certain ideas concerning his diet. Who knows what makes Larry Bird a Larry Bird?

So I've never bought the idea of a kid patterning himself after someone else, except when it comes to obvious traits we can all admire.

If I had a boy who was athletically inclined, the first thing I would do is see that he had the proper exposure to his game. In basketball that might mean banging heads on a playground, getting in extra time at the gym—and, most of all, hoping he finds a good high school coach! The wrong high school coach can ruin the whole thing.

There's pressure on every coach to win, even at the

high school level. So what does he do? He plays to win, too often without any regard for his kids' development. He gets all caught up in playing zones and possession ball, which means his kids have no chance for self-expression, no chance to exhibit and develop whatever gifts they might have. He tells them to hold the ball, play a little zone and hang in there; that way you don't get beaten too badly—and, who knows, you might even put on a little spurt at the end and win your share of games.

That might be good for the coach, but it's terrible for the kid. This is why I have such a high regard for Mike Jarvis, who coached Patrick Ewing in high school right across the river from Boston Garden in Cambridge. He's a great example of what I'm talking about. He made that kid fundamentally sound by playing a lot of man-to-man. That meant Ewing had to develop his lateral movements, his up-and-down movements, and he had to race all over the court. He wasn't allowed to stand in one spot like some dumb oaf, waiting for everyone else to come to him. He was forced to develop mobility and agility, which was then further enhanced by the magnificent job John Thompson did with him at Georgetown.

You can face the same problems at the college level. How would you like to travel 3,000 miles to scout a kid you've heard about, only to get there and watch him play a zone? He takes two steps in each direction, then holds the ball on offense. Meanwhile, his coach is building a reputation as a great defensive genius! The poor kid stands around playing catch all night, waiting for a chance every once in a while to show he can do something with the ball.

Thanks to "geniuses" like that, there have been lots of kids who were worse players when they graduated than they were when they entered college.

If a kid's got the talent, he's got to go someplace where they'll give him freedom of expression. I keep using that term because it means having a chance to develop your moves. You don't want to go to a program which won't let you run, won't let you break, won't let you play the damn game. You've got to go to a school where you're going to receive good coaching.

I don't mean to knock other schools. It's just that some programs lean more toward development by virtue of their schedules and the coaching techniques they employ. It's the kids who come from these schools who have the best shots at reaching the pros.

Every school has alumni who'll take a kid aside and say, "Hey, come to our school, and we'll see to it that you're taken care of." But for a talented kid, that stuff shouldn't enter into his decision at all. Don't listen to it.

The talented kid, in my opinion, should be looking at only one thing: the coach. What kind of coach does he want to play for? Look at the Bobby Knights, the Dean Smiths, the John Thompsons, the Joe B. Halls, the Lou Carneseccas, the Lefty Driesells, the Denny Crums, the Eddie Suttons, the guys like John Wooden, guys who, year in and year out, send their players to the pros because of the way they approach the game with creativity and discipline.

I'm not pushing any particular school here. What I'm pushing is a proper approach to the game.

It's difficult for even outstanding players to become good pros when they come out of a situation which impedes development. For one thing, it's hard to scout them because nobody knows what they can do. They get into a rut. Jo Jo White was one of them, but he was good enough and smart enough to climb out of it and had a great career with us. But for too many talented kids, stuck in a game like that, time runs out and they wind up spending the rest of their lives wondering just how good they might have been and just how far they might have gone. It's a shame, but it happens a lot.

If I had my way we'd bring back the rule which said freshmen couldn't play varsity ball. It was a good rule, a proper rule, and it made a lot of sense.

So many young athletes get a big head in high school and bring it with them to college. It's easy to see why. They're so adulated, they receive so many pats on the back, that they think they're already pros when they're 17 years old. Some of them come out of college feeling the same way. That's why, when I was coaching, I'd make the rookies carry towels and ballbags during the exhibition season. Now, of course, they've got rules against something like that, but I thought it was a great idea. What's wrong with telling a guy he has to pay his dues?

Well, the same thing goes with college ball. I think a kid should pay his dues there, too, including in the classroom. Let him learn how to become a varsity player. That used to be the duty of all the assistant coaches: To see to it that the freshmen became sophomores.

No more. Now kids are so big in high school that they're promised just about everything by the college coach: "Come with us, son, and you'll start every game!" Obviously that can't be true if he's telling it to six kids, to say nothing of the veterans already on his club. The kid comes, and now he's told: "You'll get your chance." He's perplexed: "They lied to me!" But he's stuck. Where can he go? If he transfers he gets the stigma of being a tramp athlete, plus the fact that he'll have to sit out a year.

The answer? Freshmen ball. Make it a rule that freshmen must play freshmen ball. Then if they're good enough to start for the varsity, fine, their time will come.

The thing to realize, if you're young and hoping to make it to the pros someday, is that you're probably going to wind up disappointed. That doesn't mean you shouldn't dream. It doesn't mean you shouldn't give it your best shot. It simply means you should always be prepared to deal with reality.

You want to be a pro? Start by paying the price. That means dedication. Natural talent isn't enough. There are thousands of kids who had natural talent and never went anywhere with it. There's a price to be paid. Part of it involves social mores, fighting the popular temptations of drugs, alcohol, things like that. You can't do both, especially not at the high school level. You have to pay the price of hard work, of discipline, of learning the right techniques and finding the places where they play the game properly, and get there as often as you can.

One other thing, and this sounds preachy, I know. Hit the books. Even if you're fabulous on the court, don't waste that time in the classroom.

You want to take a shot at pro ball? Go to it. But be smart about it. Don't put all of your eggs into one basket. Every good play in basketball has at least one other option, because things don't always go the way we plan, even if we hold up our end of the bargain. No play is any good if it doesn't have an option. It's the same way with life.

Here's what to tell yourself: "I'm gonna give pro ball a shot, but if I don't make it, hey, at least I've got my degree. I can get a job teaching, or a job in industry . . ."

That's being smart. Don't make the mistake of reading your own write-ups, of listening to all of the people who tell you how wonderful you are. You may *be* wonderful, but never forget that there are thousands out there just as hungry as you are, just as talented as you are, and they have their dreams, too. You may not get the breaks. Or maybe you'll get drafted by the wrong organization. It happens.

I've seen it happen. A kid sees only one thing—his dream—and then one day the bubble bursts. All of a sudden he's floundering, and the next thing you know he's taking up drinking or drugs. That's happened to too many kids who started out with great natural talent and a dream.

If you make it, fine. Wonderful. But if it isn't in the cards, don't dilly-dally. Be prepared to hang 'em up and get on with the rest of your life, satisfied you gave it the best shot you had.

Ambition's all right. It's good, in fact, as long is it doesn't wreck your life or change your personality.

Watch guys climbing the corporate ladder and you'll see what I mean. A kid wants to get ahead, so he invites the boss to dinner, and without realizing it, even though he's got legitimate talents of his own, he becomes a stooge. I'm not suggesting that he should argue with the boss or in any way become a rebel. Not at all. But you've got to be your own man. And you don't kiss anyone's ass. If the boss happens to be a jerk, do your job and do it well, but don't go out of your way to associate with him socially if you really don't enjoy his company. Too many people think they have to do that, and that's where a lot of them make a mistake.

George Marshall understood that when he owned the Redskins and he came up with a wonderful idea to promote the club and sell tickets. He began contacting every Congressman, every Senator, the presidents of all the area banks, all the key people in various businesses, and inviting them to be his guests at the games. They'd go back to their offices Monday mornings and at some point during the day they'd no doubt mention, "I was at the Redskins game yesterday . . ."

That's what Marshall was counting on, because he knew pretty soon the aides and workers would think to themselves, "Gee, if the boss is going to Redskins games, maybe I'd better start going, too. He might see me there." It wasn't long before half of Washington started buying tickets. Whether they liked football or not, all of these people decided they'd better start showing up.

Hey, good for George. It was a great idea. But the reason it worked was crappy. If you've done your job and done it well, you shouldn't have to curry favor by going to games you don't care about or any other nonsense like that. Unfortunately, it happens all the time. It's called ambition.

Ambition hurts in other ways.

The world is so much smaller now, thanks to advances in transportation, so companies think very little of taking a man who's comfortably settled, doing well, working hard, and uprooting him, his wife and their kids. They call it a promotion.

So what's he supposed to do? Even if he doesn't want to tear his family away from friends and familiar surroundings, telling himself it's just not worth another few thousand dollars a year, he still has to give it

serious thought because it might lead to future oppor-
tunities. What does he do? He goes.

Now he's all caught up in his new job, his new
responsibilities, and it doesn't take him long to settle in.
He's doing all right, but how is it affecting his family?

If it happened once it would be bad enough, but
for a lot of families—especially coaches' families—it
happens over and over. For some college coaches it's a
way of life. They're continually on the move, and they
don't particularly care where they're heading: Carolina,
New Mexico, it makes no difference to them. They get
there and play their golf, and the wife starts meeting
the other faculty wives—a tea here, a luncheon there—
and pretty soon she's all right, too. They've adjusted,
the way people in the State Department do.

But a lot of people who move around find it affects their lives tremendously. That's why a lot of capa-
ble people wind up going into business for themselves.
They don't have the desire or personality to cope with
corporate life. That's the biggest failing with corpora-
tions today. Once you climb high enough, you get a
name. But until you get there, you're just a number,
even though you might be doing one hell of a job.

As I said, I paid a price for my ambition—yet even
so, I never thought of myself as a 24-hour coach. Maybe
I was away from my family a lot, but I watched TV, I
went to shows, I did other things with my time.

These so-called 24-hour coaches bore me with their
stories of how many hours they spend in front of their
videotape machines. No man can absorb that much.

I'll give you an example. I went out to an NAIA
tournament once to speak, and as long as I was there I
figured I might as well do some scouting. The games
started at 9 A.M. and ran all day long.

So I show up at 9, sit down and start watching. I'm
very attentive. Next thing you know, two more teams
are warming up. I watch half of that one, too, then I
start talking to the guy sitting next to me.

By the third game it was just 10 guys running up

and down the court; I didn't know who anybody was and I didn't give a damn.

Well, it's the same thing with all this videotape coaches are wrapped up in today. Nobody can make me believe he's able to maintain an attention span for two, three, and four games in a row. No way. Anyone doing that doesn't know what the hell he's seeing after a while. And if they tell you they do, they're full of bull.

That's what I mean by overdedication. Ambition can do that to you and it makes you one-dimensional.

I admire excellence. I admire commitment. But I was never narrow-minded enough to think, "Hey, I'm involved with basketball and everything else is secondary." Yet that's what a lot of coaches seem to be saying today and it's no good. It's no good for them, their teams or their families, because what ends up happening is that their personalities become very tight.

You can give up certain things in your drive to excel, but you can also make the mistake of giving up too much. I just don't like a coach who says, "This is my whole life, and if I wasn't coaching I don't know what I'd do; I'd probably go bananas."

Hey, there *are* other things in life.

That's why I'm a collector. I've collected letter-openers from all over the world. Dot collects statues of boxer dogs. One of our girls collects elephant figures and the other one's into antiques.

I enjoy that, and I encourage it. Life isn't one-dimensional. You have to keep everything, including sports, in perspective, no matter how involved or committed you are.

When our games were over, that was it. I turned them off in my head. Sure, I might have thought a little bit about our next game, but I wasn't going to waste any time worrying about the one we'd just played because it was over and there wasn't a damned thing I could do to get it back.

I wasn't one to party after games, but I made it a

point to unwind. I'd get some Chinese food, relax a bit and go to sleep. Win or lose.

Ambition's okay as long as you can control it. When it starts controlling you, you'd better reassess your priorities. Or you're going to have some problems.

12

Loyalty Works Both Ways

"That's not how we treat people here."

I'm a loyal person and I expect loyalty in return from the members of our organization.

Management's always telling players: "Be careful what you say. Don't make disparaging remarks or do anything that might create a controversy which would embarrass the organization." But on very few occasions do management people, including owners, reciprocate that loyalty.

By being loyal, I don't mean you can't trade a player or let a player go. That's not being disloyal; it's doing your job, doing what you have to do to improve your team at any time. Nowadays, agents and the amounts of monies involved adversely affect the kind of loyalty we used to see. In Boston, for instance, we went from 1956 through 1975 trading away just *three* established players: Ed Macauley, Mel Counts and Paul Westphal. And we never traded a guy at the tail end of his career when he had started to slip. I'd have never dreamed of taking, say, a Bob Cousy, knowing he was going to retire at 34, and trading him to New York for a first-round pick when he turned 33. No way. You check the records and you'll find we lead the league in the number of players who started and finished their careers in one place.

Today, nothing gives me more satisfaction than seeing the success so many of our players have gone on to enjoy. We know what they're doing because they keep in touch. I'm not talking about everybody who ever played with us; I'm talking mostly about those who spent at least three or four years with the team. But we consider anyone who's played for us a part of the family. Pete Maravich played in just 35 games for us, including the playoffs in 1980, yet when all of our guys returned for that weekend last year, he was there, too, which deeply touched me. That's the kind of family feeling I mean.

In the pros, primarily because of the money, loyalty's harder to maintain. But in the colleges, where you'd expect it to be blooming, it's in total disarray. And no, I'm not talking about the kids who go into the pros early. I'm talking about the coaches who jump from job to job with no regard for the kids they've recruited and left behind. I think what's going on there is disgraceful.

God forbid that you should walk onto a campus and say to a kid who's playing for his school: "Hey, you don't like it here? Then come on over to our school. We'll fix you up with a good job and a better overall situation." They'd hang you both. So why are athletic directors allowed to do the same thing with coaches? Why is the demand for loyalty strictly upon the kids?

First of all, they'll take a kid out of high school and promise him anything. Then the kid gets there and let's say he gets hurt. Oh, they may tell him he can keep his scholarship as long as he maintains his eligibility, but in many cases they'll make it uncomfortable for him, so much so that the kid's tempted to go back home and sign up at his local school. This is loyalty?

Or the kid arrives and does everything that's expected of him. He bought the coach's recruitment line: "Son, I want you to come with us. We've got the perfect program for you, and, heck, I've got a five-year contract myself." Now this kid could have gone to a lot of schools, to other coaches he might have liked, but he went to this school because the coach outlined a program that made a lot of sense to him.

Two months later this coach is gone, headed down the road to another job that'll pay him a few more bucks. All of these kids he's recruited have been left in the lurch. But he doesn't care about them. All he cares about is himself. There's no loyalty to the kids or to the college whatsoever on his part. No time for that. He's moving up. Yet while he's there he expects those kids to give him *their* loyalty, and if one of them ever decides he wants to transfer to another school—hey, what a catastrophe! They label him "lousy" and do all kinds of things to him, saying how he ought to be ashamed of himself.

The fact that the coach would walk out the door for another $10 has nothing to do with it at all. This really aggravates me. It's wrong.

In business we expect people to honor contracts, yet here are supposed educators—presumably reputable people—who are the worst offenders of all. The out-and-out worst.

A guy will have a good year—say he goes to the final four—and the next thing you know he's signing a 10-year contract. He might, if he's smart, have a cost-of-living increase in there, but most of them don't even think of that. All they're thinking is: "I've got security for 10 years. If they fire me, they've got to pay me." That's their big thing.

Now this guy has another good year and what happens? He wants to renegotiate. Or he'll view the contract strictly as a one-way deal. He's protected for 10 years if he wants to stay—but if he gets a better offer from another school tomorrow, no problem; he can walk away. And according to the morals and loyalties which exist in college coaching today, no one bats an eye.

I have a suggestion which would put a stop to that crap right away. It's very simple.

The NCAA is a good organization. It has a lot of problems, but it does the best it can. I think every college coach, in every sport, should send a copy of his contract to the NCAA, which would then place it in a file. Then this information would be released to athletic directors all over the country. I'm not talking about the amount of money involved. Just the length, the duration, of the deal.

Then if you're coaching at Harvard, say, and the Yale athletic director calls you to say: "We've got a job that'll pay you more," if you've got two years remaining on your contract, that guy from Yale is tampering—and any tampering should be punished with a fine and suspension. The same thing goes for any coach who contacts another school about a job while he's already under contract.

Oh, I know, athletic directors will rationalize the thing by saying: "I don't want to keep a guy who has a chance to improve himself, because I'll just end up with an unhappy coach." Too damn bad. What about the unhappy kids he'd be leaving behind?

The only school I know that had guts enough to do this was Marquette, back when Al McGuire was coaching there. When he first thought of leaving they called him in and said: "What do you want, Al?" So he listed all the things he wanted and they gave them all to him. They made it a five-year deal and everyone appeared to be happy.

Then Al walked in again, sometime later when the Knicks made him an offer, and told the administration he was going to quit.

"Like hell you are," they told him, or words to that effect. "If it's another coaching job in basketball, we'll sue you! We just signed you, gave you everything you wanted, and set up this program, and you're *not* going to leave." And he didn't. He realized they were right and that he had made a mistake, so he stayed.

We have a rule in the NBA which says you're not to contact any coach or assistant coach of any other team without the permission of that team's ownership, and if the coach is under contract you are not to contact him at all. Why can't they do that in colleges? The NCAA could easily put a stop to all of this wholesale shifting of coaches who are under contract, and it would be in its best interests to do so. It would be in the schools' best interests, particularly, because then you wouldn't have these coaches demanding 10-year protection.

What right does an athletic director of one school have to tell the coach at another school to breach his contract? We're talking about institutions of higher learning. And this is their message?—"To hell with contracts; go where you want to go!" It's not right.

The coach goes and his kids stay. They've got no choice. And what happens if their new coach doesn't honor the recruiting promises made by the first coach, which could very well be the case if he intends to set up a whole new system? The kids are the losers, all the time.

If the kids aren't eligible, they don't play. If the coach breaks a few recruiting rules and gets caught, the kids are suspended from postseason play. There are plenty of punishments for the kids, but why are there no punishments for the coach, particularly when it's obvious his word is no good?

Loyalty isn't worth very much unless it works both ways, but with too many of these so-called educators it's strictly an "I've got mine!" proposition. And that stinks.

I'm a big believer in a coach's integrity, and loyalty's such an important part of that. It goes beyond the issue of those who selfishly, and mistakenly, believe the grass is always greener someplace else. It also has a lot to do with the interest a coach takes in his kids as people rather than just as players.

I know of kids who played for a certain school, which shall remain nameless here, who made All-American, but for some reason or another never wound up in the pros. From time to time I'd ask that coach, "Hey, what's so-and-so doing?" And his answer would always be, "I don't know."

I couldn't believe it. Here we're talking about kids who made *his* job secure, who helped him win conference titles and all of that, and because they didn't go on to bring him added glory by playing in the NBA, he loses all contact with them. I find that incredible.

This was always one of the secrets to our success in Boston. When we didn't have money to hire scouts, every Celtic who ever played for me was an unofficial, unpaid scout. That's how we ended up with Sam Jones, one of the all-time greats. Bones McKinney saw him playing down in North Carolina and gave me a call. When we drafted Sam on our first pick in 1957, most of the other teams had never heard of him.

We've always fostered this feeling of old players remaining a part of the family. No man who ever played for the Celtics has to buy a ticket to see our games today, and you can't say that about a lot of other clubs. In many NBA cities you'll find very few former players in attendance, not only because they have to pay for their tickets, but also because they've simply lost interest.

Yet in Boston every one of the guys who still live in the area can be seen in the Garden, cheering us on. Bob Cousy. John Havlicek. Bob Brannum. Tommy Heinsohn. Gene Conley. Satch Sanders. Dave Cowens. Jim Loscutoff. Hank Finkel. Steve Kuberski. Rick Weitzman. Mal Graham. They're there almost every night. And the ones who live out of town will always call ahead when they're coming.

You just don't see old ballplayers hanging around like that in other towns, but in Boston it's a big part of the family feeling we've built up.

You know what it all boils down to? Caring. Caring about athletes as people. When a guy hangs up his Celtics uniform for the final time, that's not the end of the relationship. We still care about him, because he's still part of us.

And I guarantee that you can go to any of the top college coaches—the Bobby Knights, the John Thompsons, the Dean Smiths, the Joe B. Halls—and ask them where *any* of their kids are today, and you'll get an answer. They'll tell you where they are and what they're doing.

Bobby could ask any one of his kids to lend him a

hand in recruiting and, boom, it's done. That's the relationship he has with them. He's helped them when they've gone looking for jobs.

John's done that with his kids, too. In fact, when Anthony Jones decided he wasn't happy in Georgetown, John called Jerry Tarkanian and helped to arrange Anthony's transfer to UNLV. You talk about a coach's dedication to his kids! How's that for going the extra mile?

That's what I mean by loyalty.

All of your great coaches have that kind of feeling for their players and it shows in their programs. You can see that they care.

One thing I can't stand is the company that brings in an efficiency expert, a numbers guy who has total disregard for people. He looks around and says: "You've got 10 men here and you need only five." Just like that. Boom. He fires half of them. He doesn't know a damn thing about their previous commitments to the company, their loyalties, their personalities, their many innate, unheralded abilities which may have served the company well in ways that aren't reflected in readily apparent situations. This means nothing to him at all. He doesn't want to hear about it. He wants those people out of the building, and that's it. This happens all the time and it's a terrible, terrible thing.

Or you get the owner who walks in one day and announces: "I think I'm going to go public," or, "I'm selling this place tomorrow." Now new people come in to run the company, and as far as they're concerned they're under no obligation at all to workers who might have been there 20 or 30 years. Especially not if they can replace them with people who'll work at half their salaries.

A lot of senior workers, senior citizens, men and women who've been loyal employees for years and years, get shunted aside this way. Without mentioning names, I had an owner come into my office once and ask: "What do you pay that girl out there to answer the telephones?" I said, "I don't know. About $12,000, I guess." He became upset and told me: "That's too much money. We can find someone who'll do it for $9,000." That really steamed me. I said: "Look, she's been here for two or three years and she's done a damn good job. If I'm going to run this office, I'm going to run it my way, and that's not how we treat people here."

He backed off. But what do people do in situations like that when they don't have anyone to go to bat for them?

I'm not sure what the answer is. I think unions can help to a certain extent, but they can't solve all of the problems. The best answer probably lies in communication. There might be a happy medium if both sides are willing to look for it.

The fact is, older people on certain jobs have to realize that in some ways they're comparable to athletes. Say a guy's been with a company for a certain number of years, and over that time his salary has jumped to $45,000. Maybe the employer wants to be loyal to him, but at the same time it's hard for him to justify paying $45,000 for a job that may be worth only $20,000. He knows the worker, through raises and cost-of-living increases, has developed a certain life-style. He doesn't want to fire him, yet he knows some-one else could do the same job for $20,000. Maybe he wouldn't do it quite as well at first, but he'd catch up. So what does he do? If he's got four workers in that same situation it's costing him $100,000 a year out of his own pocket.

This is where the comparison to athletes comes in. Let's say a player has just completed the last year of his contract and he was getting paid $600,000. He's 34 now and he thinks he can go for one more season. So you tell him: "Fine. But we both know you're not going to be playing as many minutes next year. Your contri-bution will not be the same. So I can give you only $250,000."

He says, "Me? Play for $250,000? Forget it. I'm quitting."

And you tell him, "Be my guest."

But if he stopped to think about it he'd ask himself: "Where can I go in the real world and make $250,000? If I'm lucky, I might make $30,000 as an assistant coach somewhere. I'd better stay where I am."

Some of them are realistic enough to do just that. This is where it would help to have a meeting of the minds.

I'll give you a good example. Jack Satter, a friend of mine in Boston, had a meat business which he built from scratch. Over the years he kept giving out bonuses, as well as pay raises, and after a while his workers *expected* those bonuses, even when Jack was having a bad year. He used to tell me: "Red, it's getting out of whack." Finally he retired, and as soon as the new people came in they looked around and said: "Hey, what the hell is this? You're getting $50,000 for shuffling hot dogs?"

See what I mean?

So workers have to be realistic, too, maybe if it even means taking a bit of a cut to stay on. If the boss opens his books and says: "Here's my situation. I don't want to do anything to hurt you, but I can't afford to be paying all this money if I want to keep the business in the black. Let's work something out," then I think that worker, rather than taking a hard line, has to be reasonable, too.

There was a little potato chip company here in Massachusetts that had about 30 or 40 workers. They decided they wanted a raise. The owner said: "Look, we're a new company. We can't do that just yet." Well, they didn't want to hear about any of his problems. They wanted a raise, or else. So the guy went down to Connecticut and found a company there that would make his chips, put them into bags and ship them back up here *cheaper* than he was producing them with those 30 or 40 workers. So he closed the doors to his company, with all that beautiful new machinery inside, and used the building as a distribution center.

All of those people lost their jobs by their indifference to management's problems. The same thing happened to a lot of mills here in New England.

Loyalty works both ways. But common sense works both ways, too.

13.

Ivory Towers

"The product is all that matters."

A lot of bosses make the same mistake a lot of coaches make. They become *"I, I, I"* egomaniacs, placing themselves upon pedestals way above everyone else. They want the world to know: "This is *my* company! These are *my* workers!"

Personally, I was never interested in having anybody work *for* me. I tried to get people to work *with* me. See what I mean? It's a point I try to stress whenever I'm asked to speak to corporate executives.

Some people know how to give orders. Some people don't. Some people allow authority to go to their heads. They begin adopting attitudes of superiority, and all that does is create resentment. They lose sight of the fact that most businesses, like most sports, are strengthened by good morale and good personal relationships.

A lot of my philosophy here is the result of what I saw in Walter Brown, what I learned from him in the years we were together. Walter founded the Celtics and helped found the league in 1946. He brought me to Boston in 1950 when the team, having gone through

175

four losing seasons and having drawn empty houses, was nearly bankrupt and on the verge of collapse. Walter had his heart in the Celtics, even though he was principally known as one of the top hockey men in the country. He mortgaged his home to keep the club afloat. He sold his personal stocks to keep it alive. Yet in the face of all this pressure he had to deal with, he remained one of the kindest men you'd ever want to meet.

He'd go out of his way to say hello to the ladies who cleaned the Garden. He'd make it a point to stop and chat with the members of the bull gang. He always had a friendly word for the fellow who sold newspapers on the street outside his office. Walter's feeling was that a person is a person, and if you treat a person with respect, you'll have that person's respect in return.

But what happens a lot of times, unfortunately, is that once a man achieves a position at the executive level, he loses his humility. Now he lives in his ivory tower. Even the guys who come up from the ranks fall into this terrible trap: "I'm top dog now. I'm up here with the big boys."

No more eating with the little guys. No way. Now it's the two-hour martini lunch. It's being wined and dined by salesmen. It's belonging to such-and-such a club; very exclusive, you know. It's the big office, with all the fancy trappings, and the only people you speak to now are big people like yourself. Who has time for little people?

Well, show me a guy like that and I'll show you a guy who rapidly loses his touch for what's going on in the world around him, including that world in which he's making this handsome living.

Self-styled big shots! That's what I call them. And I stay as far away from them as possible.

The good boss has compassion, and if he's smart, he gets to know his people. He gets to know their lifestyles, what they're like, what goes through their minds. This is all very important when it comes to motivating people. You have to study them first. Some you ask. Some you tell. Some you humor. Some you cajole. But you try to understand *all* of them, and to the extent that it's possible, you try to treat all of them with respect.

It's very easy to show contempt or disregard for the person you know you can replace with little problem. The same thing's true in coaching: It's very easy to bawl out a substitute. That takes no guts at all. That's a favorite exercise of coaches who want to feed their own egos. If that's your only reason for yelling at someone, then I find it contemptible.

My theory was just the opposite. I'd try to pay extra attention to those guys who didn't play much. I'd spend more time with them in practice, talking with them, teaching them, making sure they knew we looked upon them as important members of our organization, even if they went weeks without playing a minute. Their time would come, and when it did we wanted them to be ready. A Sam Jones, for instance, spent much of his first three years sitting on the bench while Bob Cousy and Bill Sharman played. Same with KC Jones.

A good boss is prepared to accept mistakes, within reason. When you give a person a so-called lesser job to do, you have to understand that it takes him time to learn it. You don't kick him out the door the first time he does something wrong or give him holy hell in front of his fellow workers. You talk with him. You pull him aside. You tell him: "You did this wrong. Here's why . . ."

You show him what he did wrong, so he'll understand. You don't stand there screaming at him. You have a little talk with him: "I *know* you're going to make mistakes. That's okay. That's how we learn. That's how *I* learned. But I can't eat too many of them, so let's be a little more careful from now on."

Take some of the young guys who work in my office now. Great kids! But many a time they've made mistakes which have driven me up a wall. Halftime shows are a good example. I was sitting in the Garden one night and these crazy dancers came out at halftime. At least they called themselves dancers. I don't know what the hell they were doing. It was awful. A terrible show. A stupid mistake on someone's part, inviting them to put on a performance like that for a Celtics crowd.

We had the same problem involving halftime presentations. I'd be sitting there, and suddenly the P.A. announcer would be calling my attention to some production on the floor. Some company wanted to give out an award. Pretty soon every company in town would have been giving out awards if something wasn't done.

So I called our guys in. "Look, this is becoming a joke," I said. "If some dental association decides it wants a little free publicity, it just buys a $25 plaque and names some Celtic player as its recipient. Who's kidding whom? Let's check their motives. If they're legit, if their cause is worthwhile, fine. Bring them on. But let's weed out the phonies, okay?"

That's a small example what I mean by explaining things rather than jumping all over someone.

The good boss is also visible. If it's a department store he's running, I'm not suggesting that he should be out on the floor all day long. But at least once a day, for a half-hour or so, he should walk the building. He should let the people who work there know who he is, and he should know who they are.

I don't mean snooping. People aren't stupid. They catch on quickly. If that's what he's up to, they'll learn when to spot him and then they'll just make it a point to look busy when he's around.

That's not the purpose of it. The purpose is to get to know your people as people, rather than knowing them as numbers. It goes back to what I said before. You want to have a feel and a regard for the people in your organization; you don't want to lose your touch.

The executive who becomes *The Boss*, who suddenly changes his whole personality, who tells the people below him that he's left them by the wayside, that they're all gonzo in his eyes now that he's become so important—that guy's a failure as an administrator, at least in my eyes.

What he should want to do is motivate through admiration and respect. If people admire your knowledge and respect the fact that you worked your way up to that position, they'll produce for you. But they'll never produce as well if your whole approach is to motivate them through fear.

If that's your idea of strong leadership, then they'll do just enough to please you and not a damn thing more. They'll see you coming, so they'll start fixing up the racks. Or if they're walking through the store and they see you up ahead, they'll pick up that piece of paper they see lying on the floor. But if you're not around, they won't touch it. That's someone else's department now. See what I mean?

You haven't won the loyalty of that worker; all you've got is a guy who's producing out of fear, and that's not what good leadership's all about.

The most important aspect of any business is its product. That's what it's all about. That's what you're selling to the public.

Everything else is correctable. You can make mistakes. Your P.R. department can screw up. You can buy the wrong computer. You can have a promotion turn sour. That's all correctable. What is *not* correctable is your product.

This means your image, too. Does the public like your organization?

The Celtics are a class outfit. People like us. And I'm not just talking from a winning standpoint, although that certainly makes everything else a lot easier. People liked us when we weren't winning.

Years ago, when we were having problems with different ownerships, and when we were also having problems with the folks who ran the Garden, our fans would show up at the box office and be told: "We can't let you buy those tickets. That's too far down the road." Or, "We're only selling tickets for the next game now." Or even worse, "What do you want to see *that* game for?" It was awful. We've gone through more crap like that than anyone would believe.

So we'd get the word out all over town: "We don't run the box office. That has nothing to do with the

Celtics. If you have any problem at all, please see us directly."

Fortunately, that stuff hasn't happened for a long time now. But when it did, we broke our backs looking into every customer complaint. If they wrote to us, they got an answer. If they called us, someone talked with them. If they came to our office in person, we sat down and worked things out on the spot.

This is one of the reasons I've never wanted to sit in a fancy luxury box. I'm in the same seat every game, right in the midst of the crowd. And I'm there because I *want* to be there. If something's wrong with our operation, I want to know about it. If people have gripes, I want to hear them. It all goes back to what I said about those ivory tower executives who seclude themselves, who deal only in high-level decisions. They end up losing touch, and that's when things start going to hell.

I'm there to watch the game. But if I see a customer being inconvenienced, or a toddler headed toward danger, or a group of photographers blocking someone's view, or maybe a table that needs padding so that the athletes won't be hurt—anytime I see a situation like that at all, I signal for someone on our staff or one of the ballboys and tell them to straighten it out immediately.

You see, you never want to forget who's paying the bills. You never want to forget the customer's comfort and satisfaction.

Really, if there's *one* thing people in other businesses can learn from watching the Celtics, that would be it: *The product is all that matters.*

I think about that a lot whenever I go into restaurants or department stores.

Take a restaurant. The food's good, the service is good, everything's fine. But then the owner starts making money, and now he looks for ways to make even more money. So he starts cutting down on the portions, trimming away the quality, and maybe he replaces some of his better waiters with less-experienced help. Pretty soon his place starts going downhill. You see it happen all the time.

Instead of saying to himself, "Gee, I've got all of these customers; now I've got to keep them. If I increase the portions, as much as it's economically feasible, and keep our standards up, business will be great," he goes the other way. He's making $200,000 a year from his business. But rather than settling for, say, $180,000, and making it thrive even more, he gets greedy and looks for ways to milk it for $300,000.

In the end, he loses. His customers find someplace else to go, someplace that appreciates their patronage and demonstrates that appreciation with first-rate service and quality.

I get the same feeling in department stores at times. I don't want salespersons giving me the impression they're doing me a favor by waiting on me. You know how it goes: "Can I help you?" "Yeh, I'd like to look at these." "Oh, you'll have to wait. That's not my department." Then they stand there!

The good stores, the ones which are really run right, are pleasant to be in, and their workers do everything they can to assist you because they know their jobs depend on the store making money, and that's directly linked to their courtesy.

I'll give you a great example of someone who's never lost his touch, even after achieving fabulous success. There's a fellow in Boston named Anthony Athanas. He's well into his 70s now. He was born in Albania, and as a kid he used to help his father peddle fruit from a cart. When he saved enough dough he opened a little restaurant back in the 30s. He'd work the counter, taking customers' orders, then dash into the kitchen to do the cooking himself. He did it all: chief cook and bottlewasher!

Well, his business grew. So he opened a second restaurant. Then a third. He's got four of them now, I think, including Pier IV, located right at the water on the city's edge. It's been voted the best restaurant in the country every year for at least the past 10 years in a row. It's a magnificent place.

Jimmy's Harborside down the street is the same kind of an operation. Jimmy Doulous, the guy who built it, is dead now, but he was the same kind of dedicated worker Anthony was. He was an immigrant from Greece who started out from scratch. Today his restaurant is a showplace, too.

Guys like Anthony and Jimmy, once they have it made, could just sit back, relax, take long vacations, delegate responsibility to other people—but no, they're *still* in the kitchen, talking with the chefs, not interfering, but keeping a constant eye on the quality of food that's being served. And then they're out mingling with the customers, getting to know them, and making sure again that everything's done to perfection.

One day I said to Anthony: "What do you do for a vacation?"

He pointed to the dining room and smiled. "Red," he said, "this *is* my vacation!"

See what I mean? He's never lost his touch. He still cares passionately about the product. That's the mark of a real pro.

Lee Iacocca is another great example.

He came up the hard way, too. He didn't come from affluent parents and ritzy schools and everything else that goes with a privileged life. No way.

And that's what made him the great success he is today. He knows the guys on the streets because *he's* a guy from the streets, and he made up his mind to find out what the people wanted and then he gave it to them. To hell with what some committee up in the ivory towers wanted! *Let's find out what the people want!* He did, and that's where the Mustang came from. That was *his* baby. What an idea!

This is what gets me. Let's talk about Ford for a minute. They have a great little car like the old sporty Thunderbird. Then all of a sudden they change it. Those old T-birds are classics today. So why did they do it? Why did they kill it? What did they gain by making the Thunderbird into a sedan when they already had the Mercury, which was a sedan, and the LTD, which is also a sedan?

What the hell was the point of taking a unique car

like the Thunderbird, a wonderful success, and replacing it with something that was very common? If there was ever an example of what happens when people move into their ivory towers and lose all touch with the product, that had to be it. Sheer stupidity.

I'm not suggesting you have to go out into the public and take surveys every time you want to make a decision. But if you're making a decision like that one, I think you'd want to have people stopping into bars and places like that, asking the guys on the street: "What kind of car do you drive? What kid of car would you like?" Stuff like that. Get a *feel* for what the customer is thinking.

Sure, I'm sitting behind this big desk and someone asks me which car I think is best, I'm going to tell him a Lincoln. But what about the guy down there on the streets? What does *he* think? Does anyone bother to ask him?

This is where Iacocca was so smart. He didn't listen to the self-styled big shots. He didn't sit back in his opulent office, with his feet up on the desk, telling himself that he had all the answers, that he was smarter than all of the so-called little people. He got off his can and did some homework. He knew something about the little guy out there on the streets, the guy who was fighting for whatever he could get. He knew what that little guy wanted: A sharp little car for a reasonable amount of money!

That's how the Mustang was born. What a fantastic concept. An inexpensive car that looked good! It became a huge success. Why? Because Iacocca had a *feel* for what the customers wanted.

And now he's done the same thing all over again for Chrysler with his K cars.

There's a man who understands the importance of staying in touch with the people. See, he wanted to win. It's no good to lose. It's no fun. It makes you feel lousy. So if you're losing, you want to find out why.

Iacocca wanted to find out why people stopped buying American cars and how he could improve the product to get them to buy them again. He was like

Larry Bird is when he takes a shot and the ball doesn't go in. All the while he's chasing after the rebound and then falling back on defense, Larry's thinking to himself: *"Why did I miss that shot? Next time I shoot that ball, damn it, my head will be up a little higher, or I'll follow through a little bit better . . ."* These things are automatically going through his mind because he knows there has to be a reason why the ball didn't go in. He's going to make it his business to discover that reason and correct the problem. Because that's his product!

And that's what you've got to do, whatever your business is, if you want to be a winner. You've got to be like Larry. You've got to work at the job. You've got to care about your product.

You know, when Larry signed that super contract with us in the fall of 1983, he could have said: "I'll just go out and do my job, the way I always have." But he didn't. Instead, he told himself: "Now that I've got the super contract, I'm going to have to play a super game to justify it." And he did. He led us to the championship that season.

He didn't lose his touch when the big dough came. He didn't lose his feel. He never stopped caring about the product. There's a great lesson there for any athlete or executive who wants to be a winner.

I go all over the place talking to companies about their products.

One time I spoke to a group of scientist types at Hewlett-Packard, a big company. They told me these were temperamental longhairs who had to do a little selling, too, but that they didn't want to sell. That was too bothersome for them. All they wanted to be involved with was research, trying to develop a better adding machine or whatever it was. I was asked to give them a little pep talk.

"Look, guys," I began. "You don't have to go out and sell. Don't listen to what they tell you in the front office. Forget about it. You don't have to do that crap . . ."

Now everyone's starting to smile.

"Of course," I went on, "you don't have to *eat*, either!"

No one's smiling anymore.

"Now let's be practical about this thing. All those products that you make won't be worth a damn if no one's out there selling them. And who has better credibility, when it comes to describing their wonderful qualities, than the guys who invented them? Who can talk about them with more authority?"

I think the message kind of took hold. When you think about it, it's just common sense.

Iacocca can come out with the best damn Chrysler car there is, but if he doesn't know how to market it, it won't mean a thing. So what does he do? He comes out with a five-year, 50,000-mile warranty, which immediately gives authenticity and credibility to his product. What does that tell the man on the street? It tells him this: "If this guy feels so good about his cars that he's willing to stand behind the parts for five years, then, by God, I'm gonna take a shot with him!" That was Iacocca's selling point and it worked.

The product! That's what it's all about. All the marketing in the world is just so much crap if the product's not good, if it won't stand up.

It's like a basketball team: You *have* to have the product. Everything else is just a means of selling the product, but if the product won't stand up—hey, it might take a year, maybe longer, but eventually you're going right down the toilet. Count on it. Because your product is the key.

It's hard for American manufacturers to compete with foreign companies because of salary scales and all of that. I know. The standards of living are so different. That's getting into economics, which is certainly not my field. But I noticed something a long time ago when I went over to Denmark to give some clinics, and I've never forgotten it.

Everyone drove *old* cars over there. Or so it seemed.

See, this was the big thing in their lives, the *big* investment. They took damn good care of a car when they bought one because it was such a major purchase. They couldn't afford to be changing them every other year. When they bought a car, it was intended to last them for a long, long time. Therefore, it had to go through your mind that if they produced a car, it was more than likely a damn good one.

Think about it. Think about the Saab. Think about the Volvo. Think, also, about the Toyota, the Mercedes, the Volkswagen.

Why are all the ones we associate with craftsmanship and dependability built in someone else's country? The answer is simple: They never lost touch with the product in those countries. We did. We have the best technology there is for manufacturing automobiles, but what good is it if one screw isn't tightened and the whole thing starts to rattle?

This is what happened. We became careless. We were selling cars on the basis of their beauty. But beauty's just like statistics: *Neither one tells the real story!* We were more concerned with the looks of the car than we were with its actual operation.

And on top of that, we kept changing the styles so that people would want to buy a new one every two years just for the prestige. This was part of the problem; the manufacturers figured if the people were going to get rid of them in two or three years, then nobody would give a damn if the cars didn't last. What is it they call that? Planned obsolescence? What a horrible philosophy.

Meanwhile, the Mercedes and all of those other foreign cars were being designed to last 10 years or more.

Us? We didn't care about quality. We were looking for pizzazz. So salesmen kept hitting us with all of these perks: automatic windows, automatic locks, tape decks, vinyl tops, leather seats! They sounded like agents reading off their clients' damn statistics.

But it's like I said earlier: Your product is where it's at. Everything else can be corrected. Everything else can be adjusted. The product is the bottom line. If it's no good, nothing else matters.

We're finally getting smart, and I give Iacocca all the credit there.

I know builders who have become very wealthy. They don't have to work another day for the rest of their lives. And they don't. Oh, they keep putting up more buildings, but now they turn over the detail work to other guys while they start taking long lunches and extended vacations. And believe me, it shows. It shows in the costs and it shows in the construction.

The good ones would never do that; they'd get out of the business first. But as long as they're in it, no matter how wealthy they are, they're out there on that job every day asking: "Hey, what's going on here? What's that ton of copper doing over there?" They know what's happening. They haven't lost their touch.

I know guys like that. They've saved hundreds of thousands of dollars just by maintaining that personal touch—plus, their work was done better.

A good example of what I'm talking about was the Nassau County Coliseum. They spent millions of dollars to build that joint—and what happened?

First, they forgot to include a box office. And the training room was across the hall from the dressing rooms, meaning if an athlete needed a treatment after a game he had to wrap a towel around himself and make his way through the exiting customers crowded in the hallway. The electrical outlets were put in the wrong places. If all of that wasn't enough, they put the main exits at halfcourt, or by the red line in hockey! This meant losing hundreds of top-priced seats on both sides of the building. When they realized what they'd done, after the place had been in operation for a while, they filled in those areas with permanent seating and built new exits in the corners where they should have been in the first place.

I could go on and on with examples like that. But the point should be obvious. I'm not an architect. I'm not a designer. But, damn it, all I'm talking about here are executives who fail to use everyday common sense.

If you want to build an arena, what's the first thing

you should do? Visit some existing arenas. Talk with the people who run them, the people who play in them, the people who pay to watch events in them. Study them. Then say: "I like your building, but what are some of the mistakes you've made here? Could I see your plans?"

Look at different buildings. Then look at your land. Which type of building would be best suited for you?

But no, that's not how it's done. Instead, the executives in their ivory towers go out and hire an architect. Maybe he should be doing all of this, too, but he's got his own ego. So he comes up with a *new* plan. He's asking himself: "Should we have balconies, and how should they look?" Meanwhile, he's forgetting all about the damn box office!

It's unbelievable. No box office. No training room next to the dressing rooms.

Of course, at the Nassau Coliseum you were dealing with a political situation, and that can present a whole new set of problems. Now you're talking about bureaucrats on the mayor's staff, or the county commissioner's staff, or whatever. What do they know? So they go and hire an architect who may know how to construct a building, but who hasn't got a clue as to the inner workings of it once the teams move in.

If they'd only do their homework, they could profit from other people's mistakes. And if someone else had a good idea, they could do what a smart coach does and steal it. They'd end up with a super arena.

This gets right down to basic details, like the selection of the seats. Your ivory tower guy is making what he considers the *major* decision: What color should they be? What he should be asking himself is: "*What size should they be?*" This never even occurs to him, though it certainly would have crossed his mind if he'd ever spent a night or two sitting in the stands with his customers, finding out first hand what they might recommend.

Let's say a regular seat is 18 inches wide. But the architect figures he can squeeze an extra body into every row by putting in seats that are only 16 inches wide. "Fine," he's told. "Good thinking. Go ahead."

But what about the customer who's going to be buying the tickets? He doesn't give a damn about the color of the seats. All he's looking for is comfort and a good view of the game.

These people who are making the decisions, have they ever sat in a 16-inch seat? Or do they do all their watching from a luxury box, assuming they go to games at all? Do they know how terrible some of these plastic molded seats are? Do they understand that you can't turn in them because they don't have any give?

This is what I mean by not having a *feel* for the product.

If some of these jerks in their ivory towers would spend just one night visiting and talking with their customers, they'd never come up with some of their crazy notions and ideas.

Common sense. That's all we're talking about here. You've got to care about your product.

14.

The Road to Brotherhood

"Racism, by definition, is illogical."

The Red Sox used to host an annual interfaith brother-hood breakfast in their clubhouse dining room up on the roof of Fenway Park, and one morning, after listening to all of the speeches, my friend Dick O'Connell, who was the team's GM at the time, got up and made a little speech of his own which went like this:

"Gentlemen, here we are in a sports environment, talking about brotherhood; how, on the great battle-fields of war, kids fought side by side with no regard for the other fellow's race or religion. That's fine, but may I suggest that the best example of what we're talking about can be found right down the street. There you'll find a team of blacks and whites, Catholics and Protestants, who are coached by a Jew, and they've been champions for a long, long time now. Everyone's running around looking for theories, looking for things that happened in the past which might shed light on problems we face today. But the best illustration of all is right in front of our eyes. Just look at the Celtics."

Bill Russell said pretty much the same thing in his autobiography, *Go Up for Glory*, when he wrote:

. . . black, white, religious, irreligious, we somehow put together a rather unique example of Americans—a mixed team of men who, in 48 tumultuous minutes of play, could survive it all and go on to win championship after championship.

There were Jews, Catholics, Protestants, agnostics, white men, black men. The one thing we had in common was an Irish name. The Celtics.

Believe me. We did the Irish name proud. Through it all . . . we never had a clique, we never had a quarrel. A man might be a black superstar or a white superstar. It made no difference. You might see me, the bomb-thrower, out one night with whites, another night with Negroes, a third night with whites and Negroes. We never considered it unusual. We simply considered ourselves a proud group of men who bore the distinction of being something no one else could be in our sport—the champions of the world.

Sports have, through the process of time, gone a long way toward eliminating problems of racism and religious intolerance. On most teams today they don't care if a guy's Jewish, Mormon, Baptist or Episcopalian. He's a *player!*

You'll see evidence of this when scuffles break out: The white guy coming to the aid of his black teammates; the black guy coming to the aid of his white teammates. The camaraderie they share is rooted in the fact they're a *team;* that's their common identity—it's *our* team against *their* team. You look at the guy standing next to you in the huddle, or in the warmup drill, and you don't care what he is or where he comes from. You just see the uniform and it tells you: "He represents what I represent; therefore, we play as one and we act as one, and if there's any altercation out here tonight, I'm on *his* side. Not on the side of black, or yellow, or white. I'm on his side, and he's on my side."

That's one of the great lessons we can learn from sports. I think sports have shown leadership here, and in some ways it's carried over to the fans. I'm talking about the sophisticated fan—not the wooly-eyed fanatic—who'll watch games and find himself admiring different performers for their deeds, their accomplishments, their actions, with no consideration at all for their race or religion. Doctor J! Larry Bird! What's color got to do with their greatness? Absolutely nothing. And you can tell that by the cheers and respect they get in cities all over the league.

This helps, in my opinion, to relieve some of the tensions that persist outside of the game. It may not do much to soften the attitudes of rednecks and militants, but for the millions of other people who go to games or watch them on TV, this constant exposure to teamwork—to men putting aside all differences and working together toward a common goal—has to have a beneficial effect.

From time to time I've been asked to speak out against racism. When Boston was going through the early stages of its busing crisis, with the whole country watching the uproar every night on the evening news, I was asked to get involved—to make a statement, make a speech, make an appearance, put in my two cents' worth somehow.

I was reluctant to do that for a couple of reasons. It's such a sensitive area, and I never wanted to come across as The Great White Father who had all of the answers. I *don't* have all of the answers.

Sure, you can go around preaching how wonderful it is to be broadminded. That takes no guts. Who's going to knock you for that? It's a simplistic approach which says nothing about specific situations.

You marry out of your religion today and most people don't even give it a thought. Years back, however, it would have split whole families apart. I think the time will come when no one will think it's a big deal for people to marry outside of their race—but if you're talking about that proposition today, who knows what the reaction of the average guy would be? He might *think* he knows how he would feel, but does he really know?

I'd like to think I know how I would feel.

People, to a large extent, are products of their environments, and it's a tricky thing to stand up in front of them and tell them how you think they should feel. They might tell you it's none of your damn business how they feel, and in a way they would be right.

It's too easy to generalize, to deal in theories. That's what most people who see themselves as experts in these matters do. They spend a lot of time theorizing. But I don't feel comfortable theorizing, unless we're talking basketball.

In sensitive areas like racial relations, I'd rather deal with specific situations, grabbing hold of them and seeing what triggered the problem. Then, maybe, you can work out a solution to the problem by showing someone where his thinking is in error, or perhaps pointing out another view he hadn't considered.

Racism, by definition, is illogical.

There was a good line about this in a song Kris Kristofferson did about how everyone needs someone to look down on and feel better than. That might be the answer. Most of your prejudiced people are people who are unhappy. They have money, but they're still unhappy, and they're looking for ways to rid themselves of this emotion. So racism comes easy to them. Through expressions of hatred they can draw attention to themselves, or maybe even gain a little bit of imagined power. Then again, some people have these feelings because they were brought up being told that blacks are inferior, or all whites are honkies, or no Jew can be trusted, whatever it is. It's all crap.

Rich people have these feelings, too, but they don't usually make them public the way poorer people do. Instead, they'll donate money to causes fostering their personal prejudices, perpetuating situations which they otherwise profess to deplore.

How do you stop it from happening? I don't know. I don't have the answers. Pass laws? Sure, you can do that. It will help treat the symptoms, but it won't cure the disease. And that's what you want to do; you want to wipe out the sickness.

Sports aren't the complete answer, but I think they've helped.

Satch Sanders made an observation once that really got to me. He was talking about people who think black athletes ought to be "grateful" for the huge sums of money they're making, as if that money somehow meant these players shouldn't knock the white establishment.

"You can't equate human decency and respect with dollars," Satch said, "because no amount of money can deal with that. If I was a millionaire walking down the street and the attitude of America was *'kill all niggers!'* would I be dead? As sure as I'm black I'd be dead, even though I had dollars streaming from every pocket."

I thought about that when Satch bought a house in Newton—a very affluent, liberal area just outside of Boston—and had people coming by in cars late at night, telling him to get out!

I thought about it when Luis Tiant—then a tremendously popular Red Sox pitcher—tried to buy a home in Milton, another supposedly enlightened area just outside of Boston, and was stonewalled by the realtor who feared his business would be hurt if he assisted in the purchase.

Remember now, we're talking about two black athletes who were extremely popular. If they were having trouble, what kind of trouble were nameless black guys having? It made you stop and wonder.

KC Jones was once honored by the town he lived in here. Then he moved to a bigger house in a different part of that same town and his new neighbors were up in arms!

Wayne Embry had an awful problem with a neighbor of his when he first came to us. You wouldn't believe how this guy kept harassing him. I finally said: "Wayne, if I were your size, I'd grab that jerk by the

back of his neck and toss him over the fence!" "Nah,"
he said. "You can't do that, Red." He ended up moving.

KC, Embry—guys who were helping us win world
championships! Not welcome as a next-door neighbor?

Something's terribly wrong there.

Russell, over the years, has taken a lot of heat for
the negative things he's had to say about the racial
climate of Boston. He's never given me specific in-
stances of things which outraged him, yet knowing
him, and knowing of some of the experiences some of
our other guys have encountered, I'd have to conclude
he's probably been right in most of his criticism—though
being the very opinionated tough guy he is, I'd also
have to say he hasn't done much to alleviate the tension.

When he joined us in 1956 he was the only black
guy on the team, and the whole city was madly in love
with Cousy, the local, colorful, white All-American hero
from nearby Holy Cross. Russell had none of that stuff
going for him, plus the great defensive skills he brought
with him didn't have the same crowd-pleasing effects of
those behind-the-neck passes Cousy used to throw.

Russell had a great respect for Cousy as a passer,
as a playmaker, as a fast-break guy who kept the team
moving, and no one denied that Cooz deserved all of
the publicity he got. But, damn it, Russ was doing just
as many great things out there, yet sometimes you got
the impression no one even noticed.

I often tell the story of the time we took a little
road trip and Cousy stayed home with a flu or something. Russell played out of his mind and we won every
game, but when we stepped off the plane upon our
arrival home the headline that greeted us was "WILL
COUSY PLAY TONIGHT?" Not one mention of Russell's great
performance!

Maybe that was a reflection of the writer's personal
prejudice, maybe it wasn't. But in Russell's mind it
might have seemed that way, and that's what was
important.

Remember? *It's not what you tell them, but what they
hear.* And that was the message Russell kept getting. I

could see it happening, so I used to go out of my way to tell writers what a fabulous job Bill was doing, which was certainly true. I'd point out key parts of a game and show them how he took complete control with blocked shots and domination of the boards. If I hadn't said those things, and if his teammates hadn't reaffirmed them, it would have taken some of those writers 20 years to recognize just how great this kid really was.

That, of course, raises the obvious question: Who knows what might have happened if the city had embraced Russell in the same manner it had embraced Cousy from the very beginning? He was supersensitive to the racial thing when he came to Boston, partly because he was coming from San Francisco—which *was* liberal—to an area which professed to be quite liberal, but which, in reality, was not. Only a damn fool would fail to see how that could upset a guy.

I had a very firm rule about not socializing with my players. When I was coaching I didn't even want to know their wives and kids, because I didn't want any personal considerations weighing on me if a time came when I had to make a tough coaching decision. In Russell's case, however, I made an exception. I went over to his house for dinner—something I'd never done with any other player—just to demonstrate to him that his color didn't mean a damn thing in our relationship. I broke my rule when Russell was a rookie, because I thought he might not understand my reasons for not going. I couldn't speak for the writers, the fans, or the city, but as far as the Celtics were concerned, he was one of *us* and we were damn glad he was on our side.

If the whole city had made him feel that way, it wouldn't have made him a better player. Hey, he was going to be great, no matter what, because he had a champion's heart, a champion's desire. But would it have had a warming effect on his personality?

I think the answer's yes. But we'll never know.

As I've already suggested, we're all products of our own environments, and in the neighborhood where I grew up no one paid any attention to things like race, religion or nationality, except when someone was trying to start a fight. We were like a little United Nations. Every country was represented, or so it seemed.

From time to time I've seen these great public service ads on TV showing little white kids and little black kids playing together and having a ball. While you're watching them, a voice breaks in and asks: "Who teaches them to hate?" That always gets me, because those kids remind me of the place where I grew up, and that's how we used to play. I never heard hatred preached in my parents' home, and my kids have never heard it preached in their home.

This was one of the first things—among many, as time went on—that I admired about Bill Reinhart, my college coach at George Washington. By that time in my life I was well aware that many people harbored a strong dislike for Jews. It was an awareness that was always in the back of your mind, you know? But from the moment I met Bill I could tell that this was the farthest thing from his mind. It never entered his thinking for a second.

We became great friends as the years went by, but even now I couldn't tell you what his religion was. For all I know, he might have been an atheist. But I do know we had 12 guys on that club, six of whom were Jews, and Bill treated every one of them with the same approach: They were all his boys.

When he retired from George Washington and became bored hanging around the house, he accepted a coaching job at a little Catholic elementary school, where he fell in love with the kids and came to subscribe to the concepts there. When he died he was buried as a Catholic, having converted to that faith from whatever he had been before.

I just knew him as an American of German descent from someplace out in Oregon, a thoroughly decent guy who never saw labels. He just saw people.

Walter Brown was cut from the same cloth. He'd tell me: "Red, take a man for what he is and what he does and never mind anything else you might have heard about him." Walter believed it, practiced it, and personified it. He didn't care about a man's religion or color; none of that stuff mattered to him. He just cared about the man!

And he proved that one day in the spring of 1950, just after he hired me, when we drafted Chuck Cooper from Duquesne. This was just four years after Branch Rickey made history in baseball by signing Jackie Robinson. The NBA, at the time, was an all-white league.

When Walter called out Cooper's name that day, one of the other owners looked at him and asked: "Are you aware of the fact that Mr. Cooper is a Negro?"

"I don't care what he is," Walter shot back. "All I know is that this kid can play basketball and we want him on the Celtics."

What wasn't generally known at the time, however, was that Walter was under considerable pressure from Abe Saperstein, owner of the Harlem Globetrotters, *not* to be a pioneer in breaking the color line. After all, Abe wasn't anxious to break up his own monopoly; he was getting *all* of the great black talent, the way the Montreal Canadiens used to have exclusive claim to all of the great French-speaking skaters. Abe had a good thing going, so he wasn't at all timid about reminding Walter that the Globetrotters drew some pretty big crowds to Boston Garden, crowds Walter was in no financial position to disregard. Remember, he was losing his shirt on pro basketball at the time.

Still, this was a matter of principle—a matter of conscience, if you will—and there was never any doubt in my mind as to what Walter's decision would be.

"Boston takes Charles Cooper!" he repeated.

There are no flags to commemorate the occasion, but I'll always remember that as a proud moment in Boston Celtics history.

As it turned out, we would later have the first all-black starting five in the league: Satch Sanders, Willie Naulls, Bill Russell, Sam Jones and KC Jones. And when I retired from the bench in 1966, Russell replaced me as our coach—again setting a precedent. He was the league's first black head coach, though that certainly had nothing to do with the decision to appoint him. He was simply the *best* man for the job.

I'm always leery of people who wear their liberal credentials like merit badges, and yet I *am* proud of the fact that the Celtics have always reflected Walter's belief—and my own belief—that you measure a man by what he is and what he does, disregarding all other superficial factors.

I don't go around taking bows for my feelings on these matters; it's enough that my friends and associates know where I stand.

I did, however, become angry at Embry one day. I used to give a lot of scholarships to my summer basketball camp—I still do—and many of them went to black kids. Well, this one summer we sold out early and were returning checks by the dozen.

Wayne stopped by my office and said there was a certain young kid he wished I'd give a scholarship to. But they were all gone; I'd given them all out to ex-ballplayers' kids and kids from the inner city.

"I don't have any more," I told him.

"Red," he said. "He's a real nice black kid."

That really burned me.

"Wayne," I said, "I never asked you what color he was and I resent that. Now, damn it, I don't want to discuss it, so get out of here."

The next morning, when I arrived at the office, Embry was already sitting there, waiting for me. "I want to apologize," he said. "Of all the guys for me to say something like that to, you should be the last. I'm sorry."

That really touched me. It was the right thing for him to have done, but still it took a lot of guts to do it. It was a class act.

We were good friends then, and we've been good friends since, but I've always felt that gracious gesture on his part made the bond a lot stronger.

My basic feeling—I'm not sure you could call it a philosophy, although that's probably what it is—is that you have to understand that people—any kind of people—are not perfect. You've got to go along with their faults as well as their good points.

If the fault is continued to an extreme degree, or if it gets into behavior you just can't tolerate, like dishonesty and underhanded stuff, then dump the guy! Sever the relationship. Get rid of him real quick.

But the average faults of people—losing their temper; politics you don't agree with; things like that—hey, that's what people are! They're different. And they're imperfect. That's what this country's all about: diversity of opinion, alternative lifestyles, freedom of expression. *That* you can tolerate, if you try.

Sure, it's easier said than done. But when you start out to judge people, just remember, people are judging you, too. So the only fair way to do it is to use the same guidelines for everyone.

Put it this way: I invest in *people!* I don't invest in *deals.* And I've made a lot of investments in my time.

My chief counselor in that regard has been Stanley Rosensweig, a longtime personal friend. He'll say: "Red, I've got this interesting deal going, but I don't want you to put *that* much money into it . . ." And I'll always go along with him, because I know the kind of guy he is and I have faith in his judgment.

That's what I'm talking about: I deal in people.

A guy can come to me with a big prospectus for a fabulous opportunity and I'll tell him: "No thanks, I'm not interested." Why? Not because the deal doesn't sound appealing, but because I don't know any of the people I'd be getting involved with.

I'll tell you the best deal I ever made. Easy. It's called the Sea Crest Hotel and it's located down on the Cape.

My Boston home is in a downtown high-rise now, but for many years I lived in the Lenox Hotel. Ken Battles was the manager there and Steve Hill was the banquet manager.

Ken came to me one day and said, "We've got a chance to buy this old hotel on the Cape. Steve's in with me, but we need more buyers. Would you like to come in with us for a percentage?"

"Tell me one thing," I said. "Are you guys going to run it?"

He said yes.

"That's good enough for me," I said. "How much do you want?"

I gave him what he asked for and it's turned into a fabulous investment.

The point is, I never saw the place. And I never asked to see any papers or any kind of breakdown. No one had to explain the deal to me, because I wasn't investing in a deal. I was investing in Ken and Steve.

I was investing in people I knew and trusted.

And that's the only kind of investment that's worthwhile.

15.

Heroes vs. Celebrities

"Damn few statesmen get elected."

I can remember reading Horatio Alger's books when I was a kid and thinking to myself: "Gee, maybe someday *I'll* be rich!" I didn't know how it could happen—it was just a dream back then—but those stories inspired all kinds of hope. The plots were essentially the same: A kid comes over to this country, finds employment as a messenger boy, gets a little promotion, saves his money, makes a little investment here, another one there, and before you know it, he owns the company.

Every time I'd finish one of those stories I'd be left with the feeling: "Hey, I could do that, too. Why not?" Or I'd read the Frank Merriwell stories and identify with him: "Maybe someday *I'll* be in a position to make the key hit, or to sink the winning basket! Why not?"

These were the kind of heroes who encouraged boyhood dreams.

There was Chip Hilton—I read *every* one of those books from elementary school right through high school. And the Hardy Boys.

And Tom Swift! With all of his inventions to go along with the great story line—like the electric rifle that would shoot tranquilizers into animals so that Tom could capture them.

But you know what? No one sells those books today, because no one wants to buy them. The big thing now is comic book heroes: The Amazing Spiderman, the Incredible Hulk, G.I. Joe, and all that stuff. Those aren't books; they're just quick reads, and it really bothers me because we're shortchanging kids by giving them crap like that.

I can remember being absolutely enchanted by a series of pamphlets the Metropolitan Life Insurance Company published on the life of Thomas Edison, the life of Louis Pasteur, and people like that. I'd read about someone like Madame Curie and it would just open up my dreams.

Today's kids have celebrities, whereas we used to have heroes, and there's a big difference. A hero is also a role model, someone you admire so much that he or she can actually inspire you to set high goals for yourself, to make demands on yourself—academically, athletically, socially—in order to emulate their example.

We don't make enough demands on kids today, possibly because we're all too busy feathering our own nests. You've got two working parents in more than half of the households today, and when they come home they're tired; they don't want to be bothered. Sure, they'll play with the baby until he's 2 or 3, and have a ball. But when that kid becomes 8, 9, 10 years old, how much quality time is spent with him? His father might take him to a ballgame because his conscience is bothering him, but what about sitting down with him and watching him do his homework, seeing if there's any way that he could be of help?

That's a different kind of camaraderie than you develop by going to games together. But too often the parent has problems of his own, goals that require time and energy. Maybe he's a successful lawyer, and now he's got his sights set on becoming a partner in the firm, which means there's less time he can set aside to spend with his kids.

And the biggest problem of all is telvision. The

parents have a set and the kids have a set. You watch your shows and we'll watch ours. Now you can relax without feeling guilty, right? Wrong. It doesn't work that way.

What happens is, the kids spend no time reading, no one bothers to check on them, and meanwhile we're producing generations of supposedly well-educated illiterates.

It's like we tell our guys in basketball: You've got to pay the price if you want to have success.

It's no different when it comes to raising kids: Parents have to pay the price, or else be prepared to live with disappointing results.

Who do the kids admire today? Heroes? Or celebrities? Do they pick out people whom they'd like to emulate? Or do they just admire people who've been made big by the press?

We used to admire performance. We used to admire class. Now we admire flair. Now we applaud glibness. The heroes now are rock 'n roll stars. Or they're athletes who look for ways to be spectacular.

This always burns me when I see it in our game. Too many guys are caught up with the notion that everything has to be done with a flair. Instead of just worrying about getting the job done, their minds are set on executing the crowd-pleasing dunk, so they end up hitting the back rim when no one's even near them and blow what should have been an easy layup. That's inexcusable in my book, but you see it happening all the time. Everything's got to be spectacular—something a man will be remembered for.

What they're straining for is something called charisma, and some guys have it naturally. They don't *try* to be spectacular; they *are* spectacular!

Bob Cousy had charisma without trying to have it, because as great as he was, he was basically a shy, introverted guy. Oscar Robertson had it—but Jerry West didn't, even though he was a great, great player. Doctor J has it. Kareem has it. Pete Maravich had it. Akeem

Olajuwon has it. So does Ralph Sampson. These people get all kinds of publicity and they deserve it.

But you know who also gets my respect? The players who, in many cases, are every bit as valuable as these great charismatic stars, but who never receive the same kind of praise and adulation because they just don't capture the fancy of the writers and the fans. What's more important, they don't *try* to.

Among the people who are playing today, I'm talking about a Bobby Jones, a Dan Roundfield, a Louis Orr, a Robert Reid, a Mychal Thompson; no matter what these guys do, someone else seems to get the credit—yet I'd point to any one of them as a great example for any kid to follow.

There are so many guys like them I could name—that's why I hate to get into names—guys who, for whatever reason, don't have this great charisma, but go out there night after night and get the damn job done.

Real charisma is an innate thing, I guess. When you try to manufacture it, you end up looking ridiculous.

I had a bit of it, at the risk of sounding egotistical. The cigar certainly became a trademark known throughout the league, though that wasn't my intention when it started. That went back to my early days in the league when I was just a young guy starting out, a nobody, coaching against guys who had big names and big reputations, like Joe Lapchick, Honey Russell and Ole Olsen. They'd yell and scream at the officials, kicking chairs, waving towels, doing all kinds of things to demonstrate their dissatisfaction, and quite often they'd get away with it. But whenever I spoke my mind: boom! Technical foul. Well, I wanted to have the same edge they did, and I started to notice how Lapchick always smoked cigarettes on the bench. If *he* could smoke, *I* could smoke—but I never smoked cigarettes, so I decided to smoke cigars. If you win—and we were winning in those days—what looks more relaxing than a big, fat cigar? So whenever we had a game in the bag, I'd unwrap a stogie and light up.

The idea was to show that I could do anything Lapchick could do. But it caught on to such an extent that I couldn't back off. It became a part of my coaching personality. An image had been born, quite unintentionally. And it stayed with me until I left the bench in 1966.

No other coach went to cigars, but a lot of them tried to imitate me in their battles with referees, but instead of becoming charismatic they became known as pains in the butt. They just didn't know how to go about it. They didn't know the rule book when they argued about a call, and, worse than that, they didn't know how to pick their spots.

If you have to *try* to be charismatic, it won't work.

One of the big differences between the stars of yesterday and the stars of today is that today everyone seems to be looking for an angle, some gimmick or claim to fame which can be translated into public acceptance and big money.

I'm not suggesting everyone has an ulterior motive, but how many stars today have the quiet dignity of a Joe DiMaggio? They can't *afford* to have it, because they're all out making commercials, earning money beyond what they get for their participation in the game. So they're forced to display a certain public personality. If they don't have one, they develop one, because the ability to project yourself can mean hundreds of thousands of dollars.

Look at how many athletes have trained themselves to become articulate in TV interviews, so much so that they became media celebrities: Rosey Grier, Alex Karras, Jim Brown, O.J. Simpson, Fran Tarkenton, Merlin Olsen, Joe Namath, Bubba Smith, Dick Butkus, Joe Theismann, Frank Gifford, Don Meredith, John Madden—those football guys really caught on: *"If I'm good enough at this, I can make a living at it when my career is over, maybe even have my own show!"*

So they practiced becoming personalities, even while they were still performing. Maybe that's what separates the heroes from the celebrities: Heroes don't *practice* being heroes. It's like the distinction between character and reputation. Reputation is what people say you are. Character is what you *are.*

Years ago no one ever gave much thought to working on his personality. The only thing that mattered was performance. In fact, public attention was often avoided intentionally. I can remember the way Cousy got involved with the Big Brother program. He didn't just lend his name; he participated. There was one little black kid he took with him everywhere he went. But no one ever wrote about that, because Cousy never told anyone and we never told anyone, either. The same was true of all those trips Havlicek used to make to nearby hospitals. That was always one condition we imposed: No publicity. To us, it was no different than lending money to an ex-teammate who had just fallen upon hard times. You don't advertise stuff like that. You just do what has to be done. If anything, you're grateful to be in a position to help. The last thing on your mind is taking bows.

Heroes don't feel comfortable taking bows.

Celebrities, on the other hand, are always in danger of throwing their backs out of joint.

Does the athlete in the public eye have a responsibility to conduct himself like a role model? Personally, I think he does. Whether it's in his contract or not, it ought to be assumed that he's not going to conduct himself in a manner that will bring discredit to the team.

I make this very clear to all of our people: The public is paying to see you, so I don't expect any tramp acts, like getting fresh with stewardesses or wobbling off a plane because you've had too many miniatures. In my entire coaching career, no player ever dared to drink hard liquor in front of me when we were on a trip.

The image of the Celtics has always been of paramount importance to me.

The summer following Dave Cowens' Rookie-of-the-Year season he got into a scrap at a bar down in Florida and ended up slugging somebody. Rex Morgan also got into a jam that made headlines.

I told the Boston papers, "The whole image of the Celtics is not going to be disturbed by the off-season activities of our players. You can talk all you want about generation gaps, new breeds, new theories and the rest of that stuff, but I've always felt that once a player signs a contract it's his responsibility to conduct himself in the club's best interests.

"Our image in the days of Russell, Cousy, Heinsohn, and Ramsey was almost one of awe, and I feel these players today should carry on that tradition by reflecting a big-league image.

"When they come out of college they don't seem to realize that the things they do reflect on the club. They are public property now. When Morgan busted into that police station to get his buddy out, he didn't realize it would make all the papers. But it did because he's a Celtic. He hasn't done a thing to help this team yet, but we've already made him a name by giving him that jersey, and no one's going to disgrace that jersey!"

That was 1971, and I haven't changed my mind.

It was a point that I felt had to be made, not just for Dave and Rex, but for all of our other players, too, though—typical of the man—Dave called me at home the night it happened and apologized for any embarrassment it might bring us. That was a class act on his part, because I'm sure, knowing him, there had to have been provocation before the punch. In fact, he was one of the classiest people we ever had, so I felt a little compassion for him that night on the phone.

"Dave," I told him, "you probably realize now that you're a target. Some people are going to agitate you on purpose to show their friends how tough they supposedly are, and whether you're right or whether you're wrong, you're going to be *wrong* in the eyes of the public. I'd never want you to be gutless or spineless . . . but still, you're going to have to avoid confrontations whenever it's possible."

I'll tell you another story about Cowens which ties in with this business of a star's responsibility to the public.

We were playing an exhibition game up in Portland, Maine, and Dave wanted to look at some land there, so he went up ahead of the team with a few other people. If you know Dave, you know he loves to walk in the woods. He's a country boy.

Anyway, I pulled into Portland later that afternoon and stopped off at a hamburger joint, and while I'm sitting there eating, in walks Cowens—covered with mud, wearing boots and dungarees, carrying a garment bag over his shoulder.

"What are *you* doing here?" I asked.

"Oh, I figured I'd better change."

He walked into the john and came out looking scrubbed, wearing a shirt, tie and jacket. Remember, this was just an exhibition game, and by now he was a star. But he understood the importance of appearances and knew how we felt about the image we projected.

I was deeply touched. It was so symbolic of what I like to think the Celtics represent.

I mentioned earlier how disappointed I was when Russell and Heinsohn relaxed the dress code after I stopped coaching. But even with the new way of doing things, you never see the Celtics looking like bums.

I'll tell you what scares me when you talk about celebrities today: Mass hysteria. I've always been frightened by the ability of a great orator to sway people, to get a crowd riled up. Whenever I see that, my mind flashes back to scenes from the days of lynchings.

When I see a politician who also happens to be a great speaker, he scares hell out of me, unless the guy has a proven track record of responsibility and character. All you have to do is think back to the Germany of the '30s, to Italy with Mussolini, to Cuba with Castro— the list goes on—and you can bet your life it scares me.

When I see some of these rock superstars get up in front of 50,000 kids and *own* them, it frightens me. They yell, "Jump!" and everyone jumps. "Get on your knees!"—and everyone falls onto his knees. I get nervous when I see that stuff. It reminds me of Jim Jones persuading everyone in that cult to drink that poisoned Kool-Aid. Remember? Whenever I see someone playing with people's minds it bothers me. And great orators have that ability, just like cult leaders. That scares me.

I'm also frightened by the way money can buy almost anything today. You see this happen all the time in courts of law. Money's such a factor there. I can't say whether all those people parading in front of judges are innocent or guilty, but I know if you can spend millions of dollars to hire the best legal minds in the country, you can be damn sure they're going to find a way for you to win. Meanwhile, the poor guy who robs out of desperation because he hasn't got a nickel—hey, he doesn't have a chance. He'll rot away doing his time while the man who steals millions and hires the top attorneys ends up walking away on a technicality. That scares me. It really does.

And so does the enormous power of the media, because newspapers and networks can determine who leads this country and what our national policies will be.

Who creates celebrities? The media do. That's why it's so easy for columnists to develop pipelines into a team. I don't blame the writer; that's his job. I blame the athlete who allows himself to be used as a stoolie in order to ingratiate himself and get a couple of complimentary lines in the writer's story. Oh, that used to burn me when I coached! I'd stand in the middle of our locker room and tell them all: "This is a *team*, and what happens inside this team stays inside this team! I don't care who you are, or how important you think you are—if I find one of you guys leaking team secrets to some damn reporter, it's going to be *your* ass that goes. You want to be some writer's buddy? Fine. I hope he's a real good friend, because he's going to end up paying you. Not us. You'll be out of here before the story hits the streets."

But this same thing happens with politicians and government officials.

The difference between heroes and celebrities is the same as the difference between politicians and statesmen.

Unfortunately, damn few statesmen get elected.

What's the most important thing a politician needs today? Money. And the proof of that was watching John Y. Brown—after he nearly ruined our ballclub—win the governorship of Kentucky by blanketing the state in three weeks. Here's a guy who came out of nowhere, who had no track record in public service whatsoever for that job, and he becomes a governor by purchasing enough media exposure to sway people.

John Y. Brown? Governor? No wonder these things scare me.

I've never been what you'd call a hero worshiper, but there are many people whom I've admired greatly.

I admired my father for his integrity.

I admired Bill Reinhart, my college coach, for his understanding of the game; he was so far ahead of his time. There are coaches in the Hall of Fame who couldn't hold his jock. I learned so much from that man—and not just basketball strategy. Bill was somewhat stoic; he didn't say a whole lot. He could be funny when he wanted to be, but he was never what you'd have called a great talker. There was dignity to the man. And the thing that made the biggest impression on me was the way he cared about his kids. All of Bill's boys graduated; that was very important to him. And when you graduated, he was never through with you. That wasn't his way. He never forgot his kids. He remained close to all of us and took a great interest in our lives, long after we disappeared from George Washington. I'd like to think there was a lot of Bill Reinhart's influence visible in my own career.

I could write a whole book about Walter Brown. He was a magnificent human being who personified everything good in sports. Our players loved him when he didn't have a dime. In fact, there were years when he had to hold off giving them their playoff checks, but no one ever minded. He was unique among owners: a man who always thought of the team before he thought of himself. Walter cared about people. He was a totally unselfish individual who found it almost impossible to say no. When I first came to Boston I noticed they'd have these collections in the crowd. A charity would come to Walter and ask him for help in pushing its cause. He'd say, "Sure, pass the hat tomorrow night!" Pretty soon, out of 30 home games we'd be taking collections in 28 and the customers were beginning to complain. I finally convinced him we had to stop that—but, you know, he'd end up letting them rent the Garden to put on a show, and if they didn't make all of the money they expected to make, he'd tell them to forget the rent. This was when he was nearly broke! Take my word for it, Walter Brown was a hero to mány people.

I admire excellence. I admire a cabinetmaker. I admire a woodcarver. I admire talented musicians and artists, like people who perform ballet. I admire their dedication. You don't have to know what they're doing to be able to see that they've paid the price.

I admire the consummate professional. That's why I've always admired Fred Astaire. He was the best! I loved watching him keep up with the music; there was a lot of athletic ability there. He took a skill and crafted it to absolute perfection. He was a master craftsman.

Bobby Orr was a star in my eyes, too. Oldtime hockey players had a reputation for being street guys, hanging out in bars, raising hell, getting into all kinds of trouble. Orr changed all of that. He was style. He was class. I was never a hockey fan, but anyone could see that this kid was something different, something special. He did what had to be done, when it had to be done. Think about it: That's not a bad definition of stardom. But he also made it look effortless—like an Astaire on a ballroom floor; that was Orr on ice. And off the ice he was a perfect gentleman. You never heard a bad word about that kid from anyone. He was the consummate pro.

Ted Williams was another one. He came to me one day and asked: "Red, what do your guys have for a pregame meal?" I told them they were pretty much on their own, so I wasn't sure.

"What do you have?" I asked him.

He told me he'd have one lamb chop, a slice of

toast and a cup of tea several hours before the game. He said: "I like to go into a game just a little bit hungry."

That fascinated me, because that was *my* theory, too. Back in college a professor had convinced me that your mind operates better if you're just a touch hungry when you sit down to take a test, and I took that theory with me into coaching. I'd eat a sandwich in the afternoon, then nothing more until the game was over that night. If your belly's full you feel relaxed and content. But when you're hungry, you're a tiger, and I wanted to be a tiger on the bench. That's how my love affair with Chinese food got started. I'd be hungry late at night. There was always a Chinese restaurant open, and because the food is mostly steamed rather than fried, it's easily digestible. You can eat it and go right to bed.

"Tell me," I said to Williams. "With all of your success, why are you asking?"

He laughed. "I figure I can always learn something," he said.

I was a big fan of his from that day on, because there was a man who was totally dedicated. Forget the eye–hand coordination and all of that; of course he had the physical tools. But what he also had was tremendous dedication and a willingness to pay the price. If he had grown up in an area that had no baseball, he'd have been just as big a success in some other walk of life.

I admired Cousy. He could lead a team without saying a word. I hear all these arguments as to who was better, Oscar Robertson or Jerry West? And every year there are new names added to the list. But when it comes to fast-break basketball, Bob Cousy was the best backcourtman who ever lived. He could make the plays and see the whole court better at full speed than any guard who's ever come along. He was the best of them all for the kind of game the Celtics play.

John Havlicek was a great leader, too—but what I admired most about him was the ice water in his veins. When it all came down to one last shot, Havlicek wanted the ball: "Give it to me! I'll shoot it, and I'll live or die with whatever happens." That's a star.

Bill Russell was a thinker. He knew what he was doing every minute he was on the floor. He was never a spectator. He was such an intimidating presence out there that he often got the job done by doing nothing at all. His shot-blocking was so threatening that it instilled a fear in the shooters' minds, causing them to overreact to such a degree—extra fakes, double pumps, whatever—that they'd often blow shots without him even making a move. Talk about respect! I have never seen an athlete who could dominate an entire game the way Russell dominated ours. From the day he signed that first contract in 1956 until the day he called it quits in 1969, he *owned* the NBA.

No one ever came close to him, including Chamberlain. I've never knocked Wilt's ability; he was a great athlete, a fabulous basketball player. But Russell was so much better, because he played with his head and he had the bigger heart.

Bill was basically a peaceful man who liked his privacy, and he was way ahead of other guys when it came to dressing in style. He'd be wearing his cape and his derby, and as we'd be walking along it would start to drizzle, so I'd ask him why he didn't open up the umbrella he carried on his arm. He'd look at me like I was nuts, as if to say, *"What? You mean get it wet?"* He cut quite a figure when he was all duded up. I used to tell him he looked like the ambassador from Nairobi.

I was shocked when he told me he was quitting. I wanted him to change his mind. He could have been great for another two or three years; I was convinced of it. So at first I tried to make a joke of it. He had this idea of going to Hollywood and making movies, the way his pal Jimmy Brown did. "Russ," I'd say, "how many parts do you think there are for a six-nine *schvartzah?*" Then he told me he couldn't come back because he'd already been paid $25,000 by *Sports Illustrated* for an article entitled, "I'm Not Involved Anymore," in which he announced his retirement. "No problem," I told him. "You can pick up another $25,000 by writing: 'Why I Changed My Mind!' "

But the truth was his mind was made up. Remember, he was coaching then, too, and mentally he'd had enough. Besides, he always wanted to quit on top, and I could certainly understand that; I did, too, when I stopped coaching.

And I've always believed a man must do what he feels he has to do. So I wasn't going to plead with him, because that would have been beneath my dignity, and I always wanted to maintain my dignity in Russell's eyes. That's how much respect I had for him.

And as long as I'm talking about my own guys here, I've got to mention Larry Bird. People talk about the money Larry makes, and he makes a lot—but all the money did was make him play that much harder, as if he felt he had to prove to himself and everyone else that he was worth every penny of it. I'll say this unequivocally: *Larry Bird is the best-motivated athlete I've ever seen in my life!* He is self-motivated to the fullest every time he laces up his sneakers—*more* than Russell, even, because Russell would always play well enough to win but wasn't what you'd call sensationally motivated every night. I'm not talking playoffs, of course; that's altogether different. I'm talking about busting your fanny 82 nights a season. No one's ever done that on a more consistent basis than Larry Bird. He's a magnificent pro. A great role model.

As a kid I didn't see a lot of baseball. I couldn't afford to. There was no TV in those days, and in the area where I grew up we didn't have a lot of parks and fields on which to play the game. We'd play a bastard type of softball on hardtop courtyards. Our games were basketball and handball.

But Lou Gehrig was a giant in my eyes, not just for those 2,130 straight games he played in, but because everything I read and heard about him suggested he was a gentleman, a class act.

Babe Ruth? I admired his ability, but I never admired him as a person. See, when I was a kid I was strong on conditioning; I didn't smoke, I never drank beer: I was an athlete! And whenever I'd hear stories about Babe eating 15 hot dogs, it disappointed me. I expected more than that from my heroes. He was what I would have called a celebrity if I was making this distinction back then.

Joe McCarthy, as I've mentioned, was someone I greatly admired. Joe set high standards: the mark of a pro.

Willie Mays—talk about charisma!—Stan Musial, Joe DiMaggio: I loved all of those guys. They were heroes in my eyes. But Casey Stengel never made any impact upon me at all. I didn't care for his shenanigans, even if they were effective. He was a guy, it seemed to me, who worked at being a character. Charisma was a job to him. But to the guys I admired, it came naturally. See the difference?

When Lindbergh touched down in Paris—what a moment! Now there was a hero.

And I was in awe of Harry Truman. I met him once and I couldn't get over how down-to-earth he was. He put his arm around my shoulder and said: "Coach, you'd better get in here. They have a habit of cutting people out of these pictures."

This was when I coached the Caps. We talked for a while. "You know, Red," he said, "I never played sports. Look at these glasses; they're like Coke bottles! See how thick they are? I couldn't see well enough as a kid to be any good at sports . . ."

This was a President of the United States, talking plain talk like that to someone he had just met. I was totally impressed.

Of course, in the beginning Truman scared everyone—including me. But as time went by I came to regard him as one of the greatest leaders we've ever had, and I think history will attest to that.

I liked his wife, Bess, too, because she was a parent. She had no interest in upstaging her husband or in costarring with him. She was perfectly content to remain in the background, raising their kid. I admired that. Oh, I know, the world's changing . . . but she was tops in my book; a gracious lady.

I thought the world of JFK. He was a Boston guy who took a special pride in what the Celtics were all about. He was so bright, so articulate, and he was a man of great vision. He was a hero to me.

So was FDR. Now there was my idea of everything a President should be: impressive, vibrant, a good sense of humor, a man who inspired confidence in others at a time when weaker men might have wanted to toss in the towel. He was tough under pressure, cool in the clutch—and that's what you'd expect from a great leader at a critical moment. FDR was very definitely a hero in my eyes.

So was Winston Churchill. I like people who meet problems head-on.

I'll tell you another politician I like. Tip O'Neill. He gives the impression of being just another typical pol, but when you get to meet him you discover he's altogether different from what his image would suggest. You sense his thoughtfulness. I've been in his company many times and I'm very impressed by him.

I admire James Michener, too. I met him once when we did a show together about black athletes, and we talked for two or three hours. He told me he'd won a basketball scholarship and I kidded him about that: *"It must have been to a girls school!"*

But what really impressed me was when he talked about the way he prepares to write a book. He told me he practically *lives* the experience first, investigating the background and doing his best to put himself into the mood of the characters he's writing about. He said that's why he can do only one book every two years. The more I listened to him describing his technique, the more I admired him. He's what you'd call a consummate professional, a guy who'll work at his craft until he does it to perfection.

I was a big fan of some of the oldtime actors—Paul Muni, I *really* liked him; Spencer Tracy, Jimmy Cagney,

Gary Cooper, John Wayne. Give me the class of Danny Kaye. I think he's terrific.

I got to know former Senator George V. Murphy. His father had been the athletic trainer at Yale and was a great buddy of Walter Brown's father, George V. Brown. That's how Murphy got his name; he was named in honor of Walter's father. We got talking about that one night when I met him at one of our exhibition games in Hartford or New Haven; I forget which. I always thought he was a pretty talented guy, so we got to talking about his career.

"I don't dance anymore," he told me, and I asked him why.

"Too many drafty nightclubs, he said. "I'm getting up there in age, and the facilities aren't that good anymore. You wind up with a cold, and you just can't do your best. I didn't want to be remembered like that. So I gave it up."

That's what I would have expected from an old pro.

Hollywood's influence on young people today is terrible. It bothers me that they can't make a hit movie without including sex and a car chase. Young kids watch all these cars flipping over, all these jerks supposedly outrunning the police, and then they get the idea that if they go out and smash up their own cars they'll somehow be able to just get up and walk away from the wreckage. That idea bothers me even more than some of the violence they show with guns. Most people *don't* walk away from smashups. They're lucky if they're not carried away. But Hollywood never points that out. It also never mentions who pays for all the damage and destruction these screwballs cause when they're racing down a street at 100 m.p.h.

Bill Cosby is a great example for kids.

Do you know what I admire most about that guy? He achieved greatness without ever having to say a dirty word!

So much of today's so-called humor isn't really funny at all; it's either sexual, mean or crude. It puts down people; it denigrates; it shows no respect at all for individuals or institutions. It's mean-spirited. It isn't uplifting. It demonstrates no class.

Cosby represents class. He's clean, he's original, and he's funny. He proves you can set high standards and still succeed, as long as you're willing to work at it and pay the price.

We were flying to Cleveland once and Cosby was on the same flight, although we didn't know it at the time. As he walked into the terminal these two little kids spotted him and one of them walked right up and offered him a stick of gum as a way of saying hello. You could tell he had never seen either one of those kids in his life, yet he stopped, accepted the gum, and talked with them for a couple of minutes—and before you knew it, the three of them were laughing and having a hell of a time.

I said to whoever was with me at the time: "Look at that. He's just the way he appears to be on TV. There's not a phony bone in his body."

But do you know what else I admire about the guy? Despite all of his money and accomplishments, he'd made up his mind a long time ago that he was going to earn a doctoral degree. I don't mean an *honorary* doctorate; I mean a real Ph.D. So he went to all of his classes at the University of Massachusetts, and put in the time working on his thesis. He *earned* his degree by paying the price, even though he didn't need it to pursue a career and even though it wasn't going to affect his income.

Why did he do it? Because it was probably something he promised himself many years ago, a goal he had set for himself, and, like all of these other heroes I've mentioned, he had tenacity of purpose. He made up his mind that, whatever the cost, he was going to realize his dream.

He's my idea of a hero. He's what I'd call a genuine role model.

I'd like to believe that over the years the Celtics have been role models, too.

I'd like to think that we've set standards which other people have admired, that we've gone about our business in a manner which might have prompted parents and coaches to encourage young kids to follow our example.

I'd like to think the name *Celtics* conjures up an image of integrity and class, of people who are more than winners on the court; they're winners off the court, too.

Our idea has always been to produce champions, not celebrities.

Little by little this world is changing, particularly the world of professional sports, where there's so much money around now that some folks feel it's no longer necessary to worry about how you dress, how you act, and how you present yourself to the public. Today a guy can live comfortably for the rest of his life without ever giving a thought to these things. I think that's a shame—but, hey, you can't change the world.

Yet I've got a hunch that, everything else being equal, most players in the game today would *still* like to play in Boston.

We still believe in heroes here, and we still believe that if you're willing to dedicate yourself and pay the price, you can achieve your dreams.

16.

Epilogue

"I'm not calling it quits. Not Yet."

I still get stopped for autographs in towns wherever I go. New generations of fans—kids who couldn't possibly have seen me in my heyday on the bench—walk up and say hello.

I don't know what it is—my face? my mannerisms? —because I've never been an extrovert. I've never been the type to run from one restaurant to another, one bar to another, one banquet to another, looking for attention. That's never been my style.

Yet I'm stopped all the time—and every time it happens I feel . . . not satisfied; that isn't the word; but *gratified*, I guess.

Is it charisma? Maybe. I know there are coaches in this country with fine, fine records who could walk down most streets and no one would know who the devil they are. Others would be recognized anywhere. Lombardi was like that; he'd have been recognized anywhere. Maybe, because I'm getting older now, I'm just more aware of it today.

It wasn't supposed to be this way. It wasn't what I'd planned. Originally, my big goal in life was to become a high school teacher, which I became in 1941. I figured I'd do a little coaching on the side, perhaps some refereeing, to make a few extra bucks that would go along with my Social Security once my retirement years arrived.

That was the plan.

Then pro ball came along after the war and I had an opportunity to give it a try, so I took the big gamble. I figured I was young enough, 29, to fall back into teaching or the business world if it didn't pan out. There comes a time in life when you have to take a chance. That was my time.

Now I'm 67.

And pretty soon they're going to unveil a statue of me in downtown Boston, near the statue of James Michael Curley, Boston's most celebrated mayor.

It's been a long road from that first teaching job to where I find myself today, and like most people who get to this stage of life I'm often inclined to reminisce, to think of all the characters and personalities who played supporting roles in the story of my life. I owe so much to so many of them, too few of whom have been mentioned in the pages of this book. But I hope they'll see themselves in the philosophies and warm remembrances which have made up many of these chapters, and know that they were on my mind as the words were put on paper.

There were several books written about Curley, but the one he wrote himself, his autobiography, he entitled: *"I'd Do it Again!"*

So would I; there's no question in my mind about that.

If I had to analyze my entire life, there's very little I would change, other than the amount of time I spent with my kids. I wasn't the kind of parent who would throw things down my kids' throats. I wanted them to think for themselves. If they were stubborn, if they were going to make mistakes, fine; I accepted that. I used to tell them: "All I ask of you in life is that you show respect and tell me the truth. No matter what you've done, no matter what kind of trouble you might find yourself in, just come to me and tell me the truth.

I won't berate you. I won't give you hell. I won't do anything like that—because that's life, and, if anything, I might feel remiss over the amount of time I've had to spend away from you. As long as you respect me enough to tell me the truth, I'll back you to the limit of everything I own."

I told that to Nancy. I told it to Randy. And I tell it to my granddaughter Julie today.

The public watches as you achieve a certain amount of success, and somehow it imagines that you're infallible in all other aspects of your life. That just isn't so. You have problems at home just like they have problems at home, but when they're sitting in the uproar of a game in Boston Garden, watching you while you're on the job, they can't visualize anything like that.

But I shortchanged myself of a lot of parental enjoyment while investing so much of my life in the Celtics—and the credit for the rewarding family life we enjoy today goes mainly to Dot, who did such a wonderful job of running our home while Dad was away. Like all big winners, she paid the price.

There are some things that money can't buy. Dot has a great way of putting it: "If we lost all of our money tomorrow, we'd still have everything else!" And she's right.

I saw a quote from M. L. Carr when we were getting ready to give out our 1984 championship rings. It was a good one: "The wealthiest guy in the world can buy anything he wants, but he can't buy one of these. These aren't bought with cash. They were purchased with camaraderie, with dedication, with the applause of our fans. They were purchased all those nights KC sat up thinking: 'This will work against Philly; this won't work against New York.' That's what these rings were bought with. So, sure, you look at them and you get excited, because you know you're looking at something that money can't buy."

I've said the same thing for many years. There are owners in sports today who'd gladly pay millions of dollars for the privilege of wearing a championship ring. They don't understand; some things aren't for sale. There are still some things in life that you've got to earn, and one of them is the respect of your peers.

Say a guy's a lawyer. He's achieved financial success. People say he's got it made. But in his own mind he hasn't really achieved anything except security and monetary returns. Maybe he's always had this innate desire to become a judge. He's got all this money, but he finds he doesn't need it. He'd gladly give up that half-million dollars a year he's making for the $80,000, or whatever it is, they'd pay him to sit upon a bench. Now he's got prestige that will go down in history. He'll be called "Judge" for the rest of his life, and that's how he'll be remembered by his children and his children's children. He's got respect, not only of the people on the street, but the respect of his peers.

There's nothing that can make a man feel any better than that. The respect of your peers: That's the ultimate! That's where it's at, whether it's having the American Medical Association recognize you for your accomplishments, or winning a Nobel Peace Prize, or perhaps a Pulitzer Prize, right down to receiving a plaque from your local PTA.

Being tops among your peers: That's the height of achieving your personal ambitions.

In sports it's called the Hall of Fame. And it's a long way from the streets of Brooklyn. It's a humbling experience to be enshrined, because you never think of yourself as being any sort of an immortal. I certainly never did. I just thought of myself as a guy who believed in certain principles, certain values, and then pursued them with the courage of his convictions.

I think from time to time we all wonder how we'll be remembered someday when we're gone.

During that big weekend they had for me in Boston a reporter, looking for an angle, pulled me aside and asked: "Red, what do you want to have written on your tombstone?"

"To tell you the truth," I told him, "I haven't really

given it much thought because I'm not planning on dying for a while."

The real truth is, of course I've thought of it. We all have. The first time it crossed my mind was probably back in 1968 when Dr. Martin Luther King, Jr. was assassinated. At his funeral they played a taped recording of a sermon he had given in which he talked about the kind of things he wanted to be remembered for. Part of it went like this:

> ". . .If you get somebody to deliver the eulogy, tell him not to talk too long.
>
> "Tell him not to mention that I have a Nobel Peace Prize—that isn't important.
>
> "Tell him not to mention that I have 300 or 400 other awards—that's not important. Tell him not to mention where I went to school.
>
> "I'd like for somebody to mention that day that Martin Luther King Jr. tried to give his life serving others.
>
> "I'd like for somebody to say that day that Martin Luther King Jr. tried to love somebody.
>
> "I want you to say that day that I tried to be right and to walk with them. I want you to be able to say that day that I did try to feed the hungry. I want you to be able to say that day that I did try in my life to clothe the naked. I want you to say on that day that I did try in my life to visit those who were in prison. And I want you to say that I tried to love and serve humanity.
>
> "Yes, if you want to, say that I was a drum major. Say that I was a drum major for justice. Say that I was a drum major for peace. I was a drum major for righteousness.
>
> "And all of the other shallow things will not matter . . ."

Talk about heroes!

I think everyone who heard that remarkable speech had to, at some point or another, wonder what they'd want said about themselves. Would they want to be remembered for some award received, or some other accomplishment which seemed important at the time? Or would they want to be remembered for the type of person they were?

I've thought about it a lot, and I think I'd like to be remembered as a guy who had integrity, as a man whose word was good, as someone imbued throughout his career with tenacity of purpose. I'd like people to associate my name with qualities like loyalty and pride and teamwork and dedication.

I've told every owner who's come along: "Look, I may make mistakes from the business aspect of this operation, but I try to make very *few* of them when it comes to dealing with personnel. If I tell one of our ballplayers something, then my word has to be good. It has to be trusted if it's going to mean anything at all. When I tell a player he's going to get something, he can take that promise to the bank. If you don't back me up on that, I'll pay him out of my own pocket, then quit."

I'd also like to be remembered as someone who never forgot the people who passed through his life, like the widows and children of former owners, or like former ballplayers and their families.

I'd like to be remembered for all of those things. And, sure, I'd like to be remembered for winning.

A few years ago, when Harry Mangurian owned the team, he called a press conference to announce he was signing me to what he called a *lifetime* contract as president and general manager of the Celtics.

It was a flattering gesture, and very generous on his part.

Someone asked me that afternoon why I didn't want to call it a day, to devote the rest of my life to relaxation and enjoyment?

"One simple reason," I told him. "I'd be unhappy. I'm too active to slow down completely. Even now, I go home to Washington for a week and what do I do? I get up. I take a bath. I read the paper. Then maybe I call so-and-so on the phone. Then I sit around waiting for lunch. After two or three weeks of that crap I'd go nuts!"

But this year I finally decided it *was* time to slow down a bit. So I formally gave up the GM's position to Jan Volk, who's been part of our administrative staff since 1971. I'm healthy. So I figure, why wait until I disintegrate on the job? Do you know what I mean? Why wait until I'm a sick old man to do some of the things that I still want to do?

I want to get my body back. I mean it. I was getting heavy, eating more than I should because I still get nervous and tense at our games. I want to get into a regular program of tennis and racquetball, not the hit-or-miss-type thing it's been in recent years.

I want to work out at least three times a week, come hell or high water. I'm talking selfishly now; this is something I want to do for *me*. And you can't do it if you've got to appear here, go there, show up at practice, make every game, sit around waiting for some agent to show up; that kind of stuff. That's what I want to wind down from. I no longer want the mental responsibility of all the nitty-gritty facets of the operation. I admit it, I've grown tired of that routine.

I want to do a bit of teaching, so I give occasional lectures now at Harvard.

As far as traveling goes, I've cut down on that. Dot's never liked to travel, and I'm all through with traveling by myself. So I turn down a lot of the invitations I receive to give clinics in various countries that I used to visit on State Department tours.

I've been promising my family for years that I'd pull back a bit on my schedule, and now I'm finally keeping that promise. I'm sometimes home for two and three weeks at a time—something that hasn't happened since the day I took my first pro coaching job in 1946. It's not that all of a sudden I've become a social lion or anything like that, but now if I make a date to go somewhere with somebody I'm not worried about something happening in Boston that'll have me running to the airport. If I tell Dot and the girls, "Hey, there's a good show in town two weeks from tonight; let's go see it," I want them to know that's a date I won't break.

Meanwhile, I've set up an office in downtown Washington, so if anybody in Boston has to find me they know just where to reach me. You see, I haven't cut the cord completely.

I am *still* the president of the Boston Celtics. I am still the man in control of player personnel.

I have not retired! Not completely anyway.

I just can't see myself moving to Florida—to Palm Beach, Palm Springs, San Diego, Arizona, or any of those places—and getting into the syndrome of walking around from one restaurant to another, from one country club to another, making small talk with a lot of people I've never met in my life.

That's not me. I'm not ready for that yet. I don't think I'll ever be ready for that.

I still want to be stimulated. I still *need* to be stimulated.

Retirement, for too many people, means dropping out of the race. I don't want to drop out of the race. I still feel like running—only now I want to run at a slightly different pace.

I've seen too many sports figures retire and go batty with time on their hands. How many fish can you catch? Look at Bud Grant. He's back on the sidelines. He couldn't stay away, could he?

I guess what I'm saying is that I want to be involved with the Celtics until they decide I'm too senile to help anymore.

Remember the movie *Patton?* I loved it. George C. Scott was great. I don't remember the exact line now, but there was a scene where Patton was in North Africa, on his way to Sicily, beating Rommel back and he came upon a battlefield where all you could see were dead bodies and the smoking ruins of turned-over jeeps and tanks. It was war at its worst: A picture of total decimation.

And as he looked around, inhaling the acrid air

and surveying all the carnage, he said something about how he loved it.

As I recall, the producers caught hell for that scene from critics who said they'd gone too far in portraying Patton as a warmonger. But I didn't see it that way at all. Patton was no warmonger. He was a general! And this was *his game*.

Do you see what I mean?

He was trained to win a war; that's what every instinct in his body was geared toward accomplishing. That was his goal. That was his mission. That was his life's big challenge.

That's not saying he liked *war;* what he liked was the stimulation of the fight.

I had no trouble identifying with that at all.

If there had been total peace in the last 20 years of that man's life—if he'd spent those years sitting behind some desk at the Pentagon, shuffling papers—it would have driven him nuts!

Maybe, in a way, I'm like him.

I used to tell my players: "Basketball is like a war!"

Well, we're still fighting our war on battlefields all over the NBA, and I still love the stimulation of that fight. That's why I've been very careful to emphasize that, though I'm slowing down, I'm not calling it quits. Not yet.

You never really know how much you love some things until you don't have them anymore.

How much would I miss the Celtics and the NBA? I don't know. And I'm not sure I want to know.

Index

ABOUT THE AUTHORS

RED AUERBACH was born in Brooklyn. He attended Seth Low Junior College and George Washington University prior to embarking on a career in pro basketball. He currently resides in Washington, D.C.

JOE FITZGERALD, columnist for the *Boston Herald*, is the author of *That Championship Feeling: The Story of the Boston Celtics*, and co-author of *Red Auerbach: An Autobiography*.

THE LEAGUE
By David Harris
(05167-9 $21.95)

Professional football is more than "America's Game"—it is America's obsession, as millions follow the violent spectacle staged by the NFL each year from training camps to the Super Bowl. But behind the game is a billion-dollar business—and over the last decade inside that business there has occurred an extraordinary shift of power . . .

Now, in this explosive investigative report based upon more than three years' research—including access to confidential NFL documents and extensive interviews with officials, owners and power brokers inside and outside the League, David Harris documents the little-known, behind-the-scenes power struggle that has drastically remade the internal politics and structure of the football business. THE LEAGUE is the most comprehensive—and most devastating—portrait of the NFL ever written.

Look for THE LEAGUE wherever Bantam Books are sold, or use this handy coupon for ordering:

Shaken by public acclaim for his earlier books, Ron Luciano tempts fate with a new form of baseball reporting: the dugout autobiography.

In his new bestselling hardcover, THE FALL OF THE ROMAN UMPIRE, Ron Luciano is on a new crusade. Why should the superstars of baseball, the Micks and Reggies, be the only players to have autobiographies? This book, dedicated to the unheralded heroes of baseball, will present from his fan's-eye view some of the true and truly uprorarious stories of real, hope-I-don't-drop-the-next-fly-ball players.

If you enjoyed Luciano's books, why not take a swing at THE UMPIRE STRIKES BACK, narrated by Mr. Luciano himself. In it the legendary loudmouth and funniest umpire ever to call balls and strikes, will keep you laughing with anecdotes from his pre-umpire days, his life as the general manager of a minor league team, his career as an umpire and more. Fifty minutes of Ron on tape!